Screen Saver Too

Hollywood Strikes Back

Screen Saver Too

Hollywood Strikes Back

BY NAT SEGALOFF

Screen Saver Too: *Hollywood Strikes Back*

Screen Saver Too: *Hollywood Strikes Back*
© 2017 by Nat Segaloff

All rights reserved. No part of this book may be reproduced or transmitted in any form or by any means, electronic or mechanical, including photocopying, recording, or by any information storage and retrieval system, without permission in writing from the author and appropriate credit to the author and publisher. This also applies to Amazon Look Inside® and Google Books®.

Some of the material in this book may originally have appeared in different forms in *The Boston Herald, Boston After Dark, The Tab, Time Out* (U.S.), *Backstory 3 & 4* and Nikki Finke's Hollywood fiction website, *HollywoodDementia.com*. In all cases the copyrights remain with, or have reverted to, the author. Their appearance here should be considered the preferred text. Excerpts from non-auctorial interviews and other material appear under a Fair Use Rights claim of U.S. Copyright Law, Title 17, U.S.C. with copyrights reserved by their respective rights holders.

Many of the designations used by manufacturers to distinguish their products are claimed as trademarks or service marks. Where those designations appear in this book and the author and/or Bear-Manor Media was aware of such a claim, the designations contain the symbols ®, SM, or ™. Any omission of these symbols is purely accidental and is not intended as an infringement.

Oscar®, Academy Award®, and AMPAS® are registered trademarks of the Academy of Motion Picture Arts and Sciences ©AMPAS.

Library of Congress Catalogue-in-Publication Data (TK)
Segaloff, Nat, 1948 –
Screen Saver Too: Hollywood Strikes Back

Published in the USA by:
BearManor Media
P.O. Box 71426
Albany, GA 31708
www.bearmanormedia.com

ISBN: 978-1-62933-199-7
Edited by: Robben Barquist
Cover Illustration by: Christopher Darling
Design by: www.adkinsconsult.com

NAT SEGALOFF

For
Russell C. Manker,
Clark F. Smidt,
and
Gary H. Grossman
This is all your fault.

Screen Saver Too: *Hollywood Strikes Back*

"'Yes' means 'maybe' and 'maybe' means 'no' and if you're being rejected up and down and all around and being lied to, you're just part of a very large group."
—Charles Grodin's advice to Author for anyone entering the movie business

Table of Contents:

Introduction vi
The Singing Exorcist 1
Dustin Makes a Speech 5
Dead White Guys 8
Good Evenings 18
Little Stick-Up at Brink's 29
Strange Interludes 34
Magic Time 42
Chickens! 47
Proxy Producing 52
Linda 57
On the Shoulders of Giants 64
Becoming 71
Photographs 78
Talk Was Cheap 90
No Comment 98
De-Clawing the Critics 104
Images 108
Toga! Toga! Toga! 113
Lost in New York 121
Nuggets 128
Time Marches On 138
Future Schlock 142
Biography 151
Index 154

Screen Saver Too: *Hollywood Strikes Back*

Introduction

WHEN I WAS WRITING my biography of Arthur Penn, I felt like the Angel of Death. I started researching it in 2005 when Arthur was 83 and I fully intended to have it in print in a not-unrealistic two years. Unfortunately, I had to put out some fires along the way and it wasn't until 2011 that the book finally hit the shelves.[1] By that time not only had Arthur died—the day after his 88th birthday in 2010, three days after the completed manuscript was sent to the publisher—but so had many of the other people I had spoken to: David Brown, Don Hewitt, Dede Allen, William Gibson, Larry Gelbart, Tad Mosel, Del Reisman, Horton Foote, and Hillard Elkins. It got to the point where, instead of bringing a tape recorder to interviews, I considered arriving in a black cowl and carrying a scythe like the specter in *The Seventh Seal*.

Writing history is automatically writing about death, except for movies. No matter when you watch a movie, it's always set in time-present. The film exists long after everyone in it has died, yet their combined efforts in making it have earned them a kind of immortality. Indeed, that's what you hear at so many Hollywood funerals: "Joe is dead, but his work lives on forever." This is the movie industry equivalent of telling relatives that the deceased "is now in a better place." What they mean is, "he's on TCM."

Yet movies also inflict an exquisite punishment on those who appear in them. Like the portrait of Dorian Gray, the movie you make when

---

1 *Arthur Penn: American Director* (Lexington, KY: The University Press of Kentucky, 2010)

you're twenty will still be in reruns when you're seventy to remind you of how great you looked fifty years ago.

Death on screen is a bizarre dichotomy. In action films, lives are burned so casually as to render them meaningless whereas, in a drama, the world can turn on a single light being doused. How does one reconcile the immense but abstract destruction of the entire planet Alderaan and the "millions of voices [that] suddenly cried out in terror" in *Star Wars* versus a single twenty-five-year-old girl who dies in *Love Story*? When Alderaan goes up, it's a big boom and nobody blinks; when Jenny Barrett dies, everybody cries. Maybe this is why we can watch actual war on television news without being moved, but one little girl down a well triggers a pageant from Nancy Grace.

There is another layer if the person who dies is famous. When stars like Michael Jackson, Bea Arthur, Gene Wilder, or Leonard Nimoy die, the news broadcasts and social media clot with tributes. Yet when supporting players die—even those who may have made hundreds of film or TV appearances—the public nods in casual recognition and reaches for the remote. Because of this, the Academy of Motion Picture Arts and Sciences wrestles every time they compile their "In Memoriam" segment on the annual Oscar® broadcast. No matter who they include, they draw fire for whom they leave out. Yet—in or out—each person had family, friends, and fans.

The longer you work in the motion picture business, even at its periphery, the more people you know and therefore the more people you know who die. It's the freelance nature of the business that if you make three films or TV episodes a year, and each cast and crew has thirty people, that's roughly a hundred new names and faces annually. Some of them are simply going to die on your watch, and after a while you start ticking them off as they roll by on the Oscars.

Hollywood funerals are equally capricious. I had the honor of attending Dom DeLuise's private memorial service in 2009, for which no fewer than four hundred family, friends, and co-workers filled the Veterans Wadsworth Theatre at UCLA. It was a joyous, emotional, and funny event, just like Dom's life. The family even mailed out souvenir videos. Everybody was there except Burt Reynolds, who had his issues, and Doris Day, who wanted to come down from Carmel but didn't know whom to call.

Screen Saver Too: *Hollywood Strikes Back*

Funerals in Los Angeles are a great way to see celebrities. It sounds grotesque but it's true. If you crash one, keep in mind that it is the height of impropriety to ask for autographs or, sometimes, even to start a conversation; after all, people are there to mourn, not work the crowd. I faced this by accident at Abraham Polonsky's 1999 service at USC, where he had taught. I came there to pay my respects to the feisty blacklisted writer-director (whose son, Hank, a video editor, I would wind up working with a few years later). Seating was tight so I wasn't surprised when a voice asked me if the space to my left was taken. I said it wasn't and two seconds later Harry Belafonte plopped down beside me. I wanted to say something—Lord knows I'm not shy—but somehow, "I admire your work and the contributions you've made to human rights," seemed incredibly out of place, not to mention inadequate, at a funeral. So I sat there. Similarly, writer Larry Gelbart's service at the motion picture Academy's Goldwyn Theatre had every major comic mind in Los Angeles paying him tribute. Where to start? It may sound fannish, but can you imagine what the signed guest books at these events are worth?

The best memorials to crash are for musicians. This is probably true in any city, and the tradition comes from New Orleans. I forget the name of the deceased jazz man to whose UCLA service my musician friend Lydia Kendall asked me for a ride, but it was a hell of a celebration. We walked into Schoenberg Concert Hall to find the joint jumping with an orchestra of the best sidemen in LA led by Quincy Jones.

At the other extreme, I took special pains to be at the 2006 Forest Lawn service for Roy Brewer. Brewer had headed the projectionists union during the HUAC/McCarthy witch hunts and was the most notorious Red-baiter of the Blacklist era. He famously threatened to order his projectionists to refuse to show any movie that he felt was tainted by Communism or had been worked on by anybody he considered Red. I support unions, but I wasn't there to pay my respects. I was curious to see who would turn up to praise the sonofabitch. Like Brewer (whom I had met toward the end of his life in a bizarre encounter), I also kept a list of attendees. It included several young arch-conservative political acolytes as well as a representative from Brewer's union, the IATSE, who was supremely uncomfortable speaking even the neutered praise that he felt it proper to offer a former leader whom history had so thoroughly disgraced.

All fame is fleeting, but some fame is more fleeting than others. Pity the performer who only acted in black and white movies, for he shall have minimal streaming potential. Filmmakers who faithfully and professionally did their work decades ago may have their obits driven to the back pages by the death of a more famous contemporary figure. Groucho Marx died on the same day as Elvis Presley; Farrah Fawcett-Majors passed in the same news cycle as Michael Jackson; Federico Fellini's natural death was overshadowed by the drug overdose of River Phoenix. Death may be the Great Leveler, but in Hollywood it is not the Great Equalizer. And that's just people who made Talkies. Forget silent film stars. I no longer dare take out-of-town guests to the famous forecourt of Grauman's Chinese Theatre to compare their hands and shoes with imprints in the famous cement. I didn't expect my friends' children to know Jeanne Crain or Edmund Purdom, but when they began saying, "Who are they?" to the cast of *Star Trek,* I knew we were heading toward the Apocalypse. Incidentally, they still hold world premieres at the beautifully refurbished palace (now called the TLC Chinese) and on occasion today's stars will push their appendages into wet cement out front. But these days the cement is poured into frames that lift out to make way for the next wannabe. Old slabs are put into storage. If only Lucy and Ethel had known this when they stole John Wayne's hand and footprints!

The capriciousness of celebrity stabbed me in the heart in a Trader Joe's supermarket checkout line in 2010. An unusually garrulous cashier was talking about comedians she liked. I mentioned Dom DeLuise, whose papers I had just curated for the motion picture Academy. She couldn't place the name (he had died less than a year before; see above) so I coached her with, "Oh, you know Dom DeLuise. He made all those movies with Burt Reynolds."

There was a blank stare that said, "Who's Burt Reynolds?" Reynolds had been the top-grossing movie star *in the world* for five straight years, but that was back in the late 1970s. Wow, I thought. Not only is Hollywood fame fleeting, it's supersonic.

The best way to achieve immortality in Hollywood, I have come to believe, is not by appearing in a blockbuster, it's by having other people tell stories about you. They don't even have to be true, they just have to be good. People still laugh about the time the Marx Brothers, in the 1930s, frustrated by being stood up for yet another meeting by MGM chief Irving Thalberg, stripped naked in his office and roasted potatoes in his fireplace to teach him a lesson. Or how Carole Lombard got back at Alfred Hitchcock for calling actors "cattle" by corralling cows on their set of *Mr. and Mrs. Smith* in 1941. Or when John Ford, harassed by a producer for being ten pages behind schedule, tore ten random pages out of his script and said, "Now we're back on schedule." These are people who earned the status of "legend" by actually being one. Are the stories true? Who cares? They're Hollywood. That's enough.

The anecdotes in this book may not confer legendhood upon the people they're about, but they're as accurate as I can remember them. As I said in *Screen Saver*, this is a memoir, not a deposition. I'm writing this to pass along the wisdom I have absorbed and to celebrate people I have met or worked with, many of whom are thankfully still alive as I set down these words about them. They have made my life (and perhaps yours) better, and sometimes worse, but always interesting.

In addition to the people who come off well in this book and to whom I give my thanks, other individuals have been key in helping and advising me over the course of these adventures and I want to thank them too: Jocelyn Banner-Scott, Liane Brandon, Christopher Darling, Nikki Finke, Vicki Fox, Paul Gonthier, Bill Harris, Jane Badgers Harris, Alvaro Hernandez, Larry Jackson. Daniel M. Kimmel, Gayle Kirschenbaum, Don Kopaloff, Barry Krost, Christine LaMonte, Jane Lanouette, Malcolm Leo, Ellen Lewis, Mallory Lewis, Paula Lyons, Patrick McGilligan, Meegan Lee Ochs, James Robert Parish, Fredell Pogodin, Arnie Reisman, Melanie Ruth Rose, Dorla Salling, Shawn Sanbar, Debbie Supnik, Allan Taylor, and Bill Weber. Ben Ohmart is more than a publisher, he is a fan, and I appreciate his support in this and other projects. I also thank my editor, Robben Barquist, who saved my Ps, Qs, and S.

Finally, I have deep thanks to Ami and Ivanna Lahmani and particularly to their sons Adam and Joseph Benjamin to whom I say that this is what I was trying to write every time you showed up and asked if I was busy, and I loved you so much I always said I wasn't.

— Nat Segaloff, Los Angeles

The Singing Exorcist

"**Y**OU GOT Max von Sydow to do *what*?" Christine LaMonte, his publicist, asked in disbelief.

"It's a Swedish drinking song," I explained. I had interviewed the famously ascetic actor in connection with the 1980 movie *Flash Gordon* in which he played the villain, Ming the Merciless. The picture was a silly stiff but I would have been a world-class fool to turn down a chance to meet—let alone interview one-on-one—the iconic star of *The Seventh Seal*, *The Virgin Spring*, and *Winter Light*, among a dozen other remarkable performances, not to mention *The Exorcist*. "My college friends and I sing it every time we get together," I told Christine, "but we always mangle the words, and I figured that if anybody could set us straight, it would be Max von Sydow."

Christine was the regional publicity representative for Universal Pictures and was accompanying von Sydow on his *Flash Gordon* interviews. Universal was not known for its corporate humor (despite having made *Animal House*); it was still run by Lew Wasserman, Hollywood's most respected *consigliore* who made black suits, white shirts, and black ties the company uniform. That's why the notion of a singing Exorcist (von Sydow had memorably played Father Lancaster Merrin in the blockbuster film of that title seven years earlier) was such a shock. But I knew Christine could handle it. She was bright, supportive, professional, and nobody's fool. When she had asked me to interview von Sydow, she knew that I didn't care for the picture but would be discrete about saying so during our half-hour CBS radio interview. Von Sydow was no fool either and we quickly got *Flash Gordon* out of the way so we could moved to other matters. At the end of our session, I popped the question:

> Nat: My college friends and I have a drinking song that one of us says he learned from a Swedish sailor. I know we don't have it right. It sounds something like "Hey long goal." Do you know it?
>
> Von Sydow: I know very well what it is. It's called "Helan Gor." Some people think it is the national anthem of Sweden. It is not. You see, the Swedes are a very formal people and when we go drinking, this song gives you a reason to drink because it numbers the drinks. It goes, "Here's to the first round, it all goes down, and if it doesn't all go down, you only get half on the second round. Helan gar, shung hop fadderallan ley." You keep numbering it as you go. The first round is helan, the second round is halvan, then tersen, and so forth. Also, it is played with Aquavit, which is devastating. It goes like this–

And he sang it with a flourish, his blue eyes glowing and the edges of his mouth turning up in a broad smile as he finished. Seeing him so happy, I asked, "Could you write down the words?"

"Of course," he said, and proceeded to fill a page with phonetic Swedish (see illustration), explaining how to substitute new numbers as the rounds progressed. When he finished—in for a penny, in for a pound—I asked, "how about autographing it?" He nodded yes, picked up the pen again, signed the paper, and handed it back to me. He had written only, "Ming, etc.," got up, left the recording studio, and returned to Christine's capable hands.

At my college crowd's next reunion (which we call the Extravaganza) I played the tape of von Sydow's solo and handed out photocopies of his lyrics. We tried it his way for two or three rounds until the Aquavit took hold. Von Sydow was right; it *is* devastating. It tastes of caraway seeds and the effect is like French kissing a loaf of rye bread. We switched back to beer. Tradition dies hard.

So does his film, *The Exorcist*. Much has been written about the blockbuster not only from its influence on cinema, both commercial and aesthetic, but from its representation of Catholicism. The effects on each are profound and tend to conflict. To Catholics, the belief in a personified devil and the power of the Roman Ritual to cast him out confers an aura of legitimacy upon stories of the supernatural. Hollywood taps into this superstition in its undying affinity for the horror genre. Many forces are at play in this one-sided relationship, not the least of which is Hollywood's uneasy portrayal of religion. The Jewish founders[2] of the American film industry were nearly paranoid about keeping their faith off the screen in case the anti-Semitism for which they fled the old country would turn into reprisals in Christian-dominated America. They had their stars de-ethnicize their names, made a big deal over Christmas, and built their own country clubs when the nabobs of Los Angeles denied them membership. The result—as historian Neal Gabler wrote in his landmark book *An Empire of Their Own* (NY: Crown, 1988)—is that the Jewish moguls whose access was blocked to the American dream invented an idealized version of it that the whole world came to believe. And it was not Jewish.

"Jews aren't interesting," MGM's Louis B. Mayer supposedly told a producer who wanted the studio to make a Jewish story. "Priests are interesting. They have all of that *stuff.*" Mayer was probably less interested in collars, cassocks, and rosaries than with widespread American anti-Semitism and the studios' vulnerability to Justice Department retribution for their monopolistic business practices. It was a small leap, Mayer *et al* feared, between blaming the Jews for the Great Depression and charging them with promoting a Communist takeover of America. After *The Jazz Singer* in 1927, rabbis barely appeared on screen, and the operative ethic became that the movies were all about Jewish Hollywood telling Protestant America how to be more Catholic.

The Exorcist brought religion out of the confessional. Max von Sydow's resolute Lancaster Merrin, S.J. and Jason Miller's haunted Fr. Damien "Dimmy" Karras were no cuddly priests in the mold of Pat O'Brien, Barry Fitzgerald, or Bing Crosby. Their gravitas only underscored the seriousness of what could have been, in less able filmmaking hands, a howler. Written by Jesuit scholar William Peter Blatty and directed by lapsed Jew William Friedkin (who took communion and in later life flirted with accepting Jesus), *The Exorcist* was successful not only

---

2 Exceptions include Darryl F. Zanuck, Walt Disney, D.W. Griffith, and Mack Sennett, but you get the idea.

Screen Saver Too: *Hollywood Strikes Back*

because of its superb filmmaking but because it took religion seriously.[3] It wasn't the projectile pea soup or rotating heads that made it effective, it was because such horrific things were happening to well-drawn and well-acted characters.[4] Blatty maintains—and I believe him—that he wasn't trying to scare people with his bestselling novel, he was writing a detective yarn with spiritual overtones. Yet he tapped into a primal pool of religious superstition.

It may be significant that the scene that drove most people up the aisles and toward the restrooms—if they made it past the carpet in the lobby before throwing up—was not the pea soup or crucifix, it was the medically accurate hospital arteriogram that twelve-year-old Linda Blair endures. And if that didn't do it, it was the moment when Regan's throat swells up and she makes demonic sounds. The arteriogram, with its spurting blood, was an obvious inducement to nausea. The throat swelling was more noteworthy: it is the first thing Regan does that cannot be explained by rational means. And here's another note that Warner Bros. told us at the time: most of the people who had to leave the theatre were men. Women, it seems, were stronger in their ability to support a child in peril, and they remained in their seats.

British film critic and scholar Mark Kermode, who has written extensively on *The Exorcist*, has called it the greatest film ever made. That can be disputed, but it is surely safe to say it's among the most effective, profitable, and influential motion pictures in history as audiences swept up in the cultural phenomenon of its Christmas 1973 release will remember for the rest of their lives.

---

[3] Friedkin wrote an article for the October 31, 2016 *Vanity Fair* about attending an actual exorcism in Italy with Vatican exorcist Father Gabrielle Amorth. The usually unflappable Friedkin, who has always treated the subject seriously, reports that he felt danger and the presence of forces he could not rationally explain.

[4] Both Blatty and I agree that the film goes too far in its infamous scene in which Regan MacNeill's head turns completely around without snapping off. "Unbelievable does not mean impossible," he said. The demon's purpose in possessing the girl is not to kill her but to destroy the faith of those around her.

Dustin Makes a Speech

"NAT? IT'S DUSTIN."

I should have passed out from excitement, but when Dustin Hoffman's call came in at 10 o'clock on a weekend night it was just one more in a string of conversations. True, they were with a man who happened to be one of the finest actors of his—and probably most other—generations. But it was still 10 o'clock and we were not getting any closer to finishing what we were working on.

In mid-2004, Hoffman consented to accept the Bill of Rights Award from the American Civil Liberties Union of Southern California at their December fundraising dinner. It would be presented by his *Meet the Fokkers* co-star, Ben Stiller, and, upon receiving it, he would be expected to make an acceptance speech. What would he say? Actors like to ad lib. Stars know better. Hoffman is a star as well as an actor, and we were connected by the ACLU's special events coordinator Meegan Ochs to craft his remarks. Because of his schedule, we would not have the chance to get together in person before the ceremony, so our collaboration had to be entirely by telephone. I should also mention that I am a member of the Board of Directors of the ACLU/SC.

I had heard all the stories about him, or so I thought. He was a perfectionist. He was intransigent. He was intuitive as well as trained. Larry Gelbart, who was brought in to fix the script of *Tootsie* (1982) that Hoffman had begun with his playwright buddy Murray Schisgal, had such a tough time that he famously said, "Never give an Academy Award® to any actor who is shorter than the statuette." (Hoffman and Gelbart later

Screen Saver Too: *Hollywood Strikes Back*

reconciled.) The killer quote, though, was from Sydney Pollack, *Tootsie's* director, who said he'd happily exchange everything he earned from the picture to get back the three years he spent working with its star.

The first thing I discovered about Dustin Hoffman was that he doesn't sound like Dustin Hoffman when he's not playing a character. All the impressions that people do of him from 1969's *Midnight Cowboy* ("I'm walkin' here!") or 1979's *Kramer vs. Kramer* ("No, no, no, don't touch the ice cream") yield to his soft, clear, accent-free (he's from LA, not New York) speaking voice. We discussed the importance of the ACLU in general and the Bill of Rights in particular, and what the award meant to him. "You can use this speech to put feelings on the public record that you're passionate about," I said. I raised the subject of Lenny Bruce, the revolutionary night club comic he played in 1974's *Lenny*, and quoted back some of his dialogue: "You need the deviate to stand up and tell you when you're blowing it," and "Don't take away my words." He wanted to put humor into what he feared would be a stodgy speech. I was thrilled and suggested, "Maybe we can insist that each of your films is a message picture even if it's not, like *Ishtar* was a plea for Middle East peace." He liked that and we spitballed some ideas. I sent him a draft a day later and he called me a day after that to discuss it.

I don't remember exactly what his suggestions were, but I know that every one of them was on the mark. Sometimes he took issue with a word I used that he didn't, other times it was a concept, and still other times we just talked. He knew what he *didn't* like and it was up to me to find what he *did* like. It soon became clear to me that Hoffman, like many other actors I've worked with on speeches, become defensive when they realize that they will be speaking as themselves, not in character. No thespic shield will protect them; they will be held accountable for their own words, so those words had better be theirs, even if I help them do the writing.

Hoffman's judgment was un-erring even if it was un-defined. Over the course of seven days we spoke no fewer than half a dozen times for no less than half an hour, between which I would send rewrites and he would rewrite them. Back and forth. He could change what he saw in front of him but could not (or perhaps chose not to) face a blank page. A week before the dinner we locked the text, sent it to be put up on teleprompter, and agreed to finally meet face to face at the dinner.

The day of the dinner, I was told that Hoffman had made some last-minute changes to the text. I had no problem with that; after all, he's the guy who had to say it to a thousand people. When I arrived at the Beverly Wilshire Hotel, whose green room and backstage I supervised during the program, I scrolled through his edited speech and was heartbroken to see that he had deleted so much of what we had both agreed upon. I didn't meet him before the show, but I was prepared to be disappointed. Ben Stiller gave him a suitably loving and profane introduction. Dustin got laughs with the *Ishtar* joke and a few others we had written, and then he settled into the meat of the speech, which was about the artist's need for freedom of speech and the importance of the ACLU in protecting it.

And then halfway into the speech he did something unexpected. He went off book. At first I thought he'd gone up on his lines, and so did Jamie Stevens, who was running the prompter. But no, he was using all of the material we had previously cut—only now, in performance, it came together in his mind and he flawlessly rearranged it on the fly and made it seamlessly fit. After a few minutes he segued back into the script, the prompter started again, and he finished to an ovation.

We met in the lobby after the dinner and thanked each other for the "experience." He knew what I meant, but he could not have known the value of what he had taught me, which was more than I had learned in twenty years of writing for a living. I learned that some actors know what they want, but not until they see it, and sometimes not even until they hear themselves say it. I also learned that such people need to be encouraged, not confined, and that the process is sometimes more important than the goal. I began to understand how such an empirical system conflicts with the doctrine of commercial filmmaking, but how rewarding it can be if the sides can somehow be balanced.

The next year, Dustin did a return favor for me when I was asked to host a tribute to Arthur Penn that the Academy of Motion Picture Arts and Sciences was holding in New York. I asked him if he would videotape a message for us to show Arthur at the event. He agreed, and his publicist worked it out. The message was short: "Arthur, it's Dustin. We made *Little Big Man* thirty-five years ago. How come you haven't hired me again?"

Arthur didn't have to say why because, by then, I knew.

Screen Saver Too: *Hollywood Strikes Back*

Dead White Guys

I PRODUCED FOUR *Biography* documentaries for the Arts & Entertainment Network (before they shrank their name to "A&E" and got rid of the "A") and walked off a fifth. The work was great, the freedom was remarkable, and the results were satisfying (except for the one I walked off of, but let's leave that till later).

A&E always blushed to admit it, but they didn't invent their signature show, David L. Wolper and Jack Haley, Jr. did. The original *Biography* ran as a syndicated half-hour series hosted by Mike Wallace from 1961 until 1964, then enjoyed a brief afterlife in reruns and as school educational films. When I went to work for independent Weller/Grossman Productions in 1995, they had just landed the contract to produce new episodes for *Biography* at a time when A&E was gearing up to expand the show from weekly to weeknightly. It meant an immense investment of money and personnel for the network (which was, at the beginning, a partnership between Hearst/ABC and RCA/NBC that somehow escaped Justice Department anti-trust scrutiny) and threw off jobs to a number of suppliers. This was in the days when the FCC's rules still prevented TV networks from producing and owning their own shows, a decree that encouraged diversity both in hiring and in points of view.

Robb Weller and Gary H. Grossman had formed Weller/Grossman Productions in 1993 and jumped headlong into the burgeoning cable TV market. Robb was best known as a co-host on the popular syndicated Hollywood news program *Entertainment Tonight* (begun by Jack Haley, Jr.) while Gary was a top producer on that show. Almost immediately

W/G struck video gold by landing orders from A&E to produce *Time Machine*, a history anthology hosted by the avuncular Jack Perkins. That's when I came to their attention. I had worked with Gary at the *Boston Herald* where he was TV critic before moving to Los Angeles and, when I moved to LA the year that he and Robb started their company, we reconnected. First I was interviewed for a *Time Machine* episode called "The Hollywood Censorship Wars" where my knowledge of censorship, the Production Code, and an ability to be concise on camera were an advantage. The next year, when they received a six-episode order for the launch of *Biography*, they handed me a list of people the network wanted to cover and asked me if I knew any of them. The carrot was that, if I did, I could produce the episode. John Belushi was on the list, and by chance I knew John's widow, Judith Jacklin, who had married my college classmate (and fellow film school survivor) writer-producer Victor Pisano. Not only was Judy amendable to having me profile John, she had a wealth of videotaped interviews with their friends and co-workers that she had shot shortly after his death, some of which were for an MTV tribute, and others of which were for her own archive. We licensed them and I produced "John Belushi: Funny You Should Ask" (A&E's title, not mine) from her clips. We never even turned on a camera. With Adam "Chip" Pauken's clever editing and conspiratorial sense of humor, we sent the completed episode to the A&E executives to air during the revamped series' debut week.

It's helpful to note that, at the time, A&E was not only quintupling its *Biography* output, it was re-conceiving the show's format. As Weller/Grossman had two episodes scheduled for that first week week (mine plus an episode on Gilda Radner produced by Robin Sestero that used, as its spine, an interview I had conducted with Gilda in Boston in 1984 for *The Woman in Red*), we were asked to create a style that the network would thereafter follow. For "John Belushi," we opened each segment with a printed on-screen quote drawn from one of the interviews that would be coming up in that segment and, for the ending, we compiled a montage of memorial quotes guaranteed to evoke tears. When they screened it, the network gave us only two notes: stick a clip from *Saturday Night Live*'s spoof of *Star Trek* at the beginning so viewers will know that John Belushi was funny, and never use on-screen quotes again. Otherwise, the formula we used became the *Biography* format: Open with three sound bites describing various aspects of the subject, show a clip of him (or her) being famous, flash back to his birth, and keep reminding the audience why we like him.

Although the Belushi episode was atypical in that it was constructed entirely out of preexisting footage, we hit an unexpected snag after it aired. In licensing the *SNL* clips from executive producer Lorne Michaels' company, Broadway Video, which held the rights, we included "Don't Look Back in Anger," Tom Schiller's famous "Schiller's Reel" showing an elderly John Belushi in a snowy graveyard mourning his lost *SNL* compadres. It was a perfect way to bookend the episode and I was astonished that none of the earlier Belushi tributes had thought to use it. After we broadcast the show we discovered why: Broadway Video didn't own the short, Schiller did. It was a slip-up that might have killed the episode, but Lorne Michaels honorably intervened and "John Belushi: Funny You Should Ask" aired as planned. The *Variety* and *Hollywood Reporter* reviewers loved it despite the use of on-screen quotes.

Beyond A&E's ongoing mandate to "remind viewers why they like the person," making positive, authorized biographies has its advantages, namely the friendly participation of the subjects, their families, or their heirs. Judy sent me a huge carton of John's personal belongings to use in the show. Contents included his Wheaton High School letter jacket, his collection of *National Lampoons*, recordings of *National Lampoon Radio Hour*, and Second City skits. We also had access to family home movies. In addition to Judy, John's younger brother, Jim, was an advisor. I visited Jim at his then-home in Brentwood for insight into the brothers' relationship. Naturally, we discussed John's death and, when Jim saw that I was not out to sensationalize it, he described it in a way that stunned me. He said, "It was an industrial accident." He wasn't being funny. He was saying that, given the pressures and temptations his brother was under, some sort of job-driven tragedy was inevitable. A&E's mandate was never truer: in producing the show, I was reminded why I liked John Belushi.

After "Funny You Should Ask," we were not only off and running, we were at a gallop. A&E discovered that they had a hole in their schedule and needed us to fill it, fast. As a result, they gave us nine days (it usually takes two months) to deliver another episode. The answer was "Shari Lewis & Lamb Chop," a profile of the venerable ventriloquist and her sassy sock puppet. We only pulled it off because Gary Grossman had written the landmark book, *Saturday Morning TV* (NY: Dell Books, 1982), and knew Shari and her family so well that they opened their hearts and files to us. Jean Louise Codianni, Chip Pauken, and I were handed the assignment, which was as much about nostalgia as it was *Biography*. Shari's archivist, Todd Tillson, had his fingers on any information we could ever have needed, and the people in Shari's past and present were uniformly giving. Because we didn't have time to keep interviewing people until the narrative thread emerged, I made the unusual decision to write the script first and then guide interviewees for answers that would fill in the blanks. Thus, instead of pulling the story out of the people, we put the people in the story. This was how I met and befriended Barbara and Lan O'Kun[5]—Shari's sister and brother-in-law/chief writer—and managed to get the finished show into A&E's hands in the promised nine days.

Then the network sat on it. They didn't give us any notes or reasons, they just sat on it and filled their hole with something else.

Despite this, A&E approved us to do an episode about Larry King, who was about to celebrate his tenth anniversary on CNN. We made a deal with King and the network, which was still run by Ted Turner at the time, to hang around Larry, who lived in Virginia across the Potomac River from CNN's Washington, DC bureau, and then go to New York to visit his old neighborhood. Our coordinating producer, Jean Louise Codianni, even wangled an interview with Texas businessman Ross Perot, who had begun his Quixotic 1992 presidential campaign on Larry's show. Other interviewees included reporter Peter Arnett, CNN News President Tom Johnson, Larry's stalwart producer Wendy Walker Whitworth, Larry's boyhood friend Herb Cohen (whom my Washington, DC colleague Stan Levin interviewed), former New York Governor Mario Cuomo, wife number three/five Ailene Atkins, and their daughter Chaia.

How best to describe Larry King? He's a great date. He's also in his own world. The record shows—and his memoirs confirm—that he is a bad manager of money, wives, and the law. He has a gift for asking people questions that others want to have answered while not asking questions that might throw light into the dark corners of his guests' lives.

---

5 Barbara and Lan O'Kun feature in the opening of *Screen Saver*.

This non-threatening reputation gave him countless opportunities, most of which he failed to exploit.

You gotta love Larry. He absolutely believes everything he says at the moment he says it. After that, you're on your own. When he insisted that he had no family photos for us to use, including wedding pictures, we resorted to portraying his many trips to the altar by showing a wedding cake with increasingly large chunks being taken out of it with each new nuptial. Edward Salier edited the complex storyline with verve. The CNN people were astonishingly supportive, providing access, clips, documentation, and clearances at the highest level of quality. (The only other organization I've worked with that delivers 100 percent is Disney.)

Nevertheless, there were bumps that created opportunity as well as concern. Larry has always been up front about his 1971 arrest for grand larceny, a grandiose name for financial funny business involving loans. My research, however—disregarding his memoirs and newspaper puff pieces—turned up mention of a possible illegitimate child. I brought this up during a conversation with his attorney, Stacy Woolf (daughter of legendary sports attorney Bob Woolf), when there seemed to be some question over access to Larry's family information. Agreeing that it would be hurtful to the child to bring him or her into the show, Larry's family information suddenly became available. It was nothing scandalous, only helpful[6]

The other story has nothing to do with Larry King. I had been slipped an internal CNN memo stating Ted Turner's belief that the word *foreign* stigmatized the differences between countries and had a polarizing effect, so it was thereafter banned from CNN's lexicon. This mandate applied not just on the air but everywhere in the building. Instead, the word *international* was to be used. At first, people joked, "I have a piece of international matter in my eye," but Turner wasn't kidding. For a news organization that dealt with world affairs, switching from *foreign* to *international* was a major grammatical event. Just to make it stick, anyone caught saying *foreign* was to be fined $50. If the verbal miscreant kept it up, the ultimate punishment was termination. I asked Tom Johnson if the memo was a joke.

---

6 My sources were readily available newspaper articles from which nobody else had apparently seen fit to connect the dots. The timing of the boy's birth and Larry's marriage to the mother were unclear at the time but have since been resolved.

"It's true," he confirmed. "You can't use the F-word anywhere around here." (Notice that he didn't say *foreign*.)

"Larry King: Talk of Fame" (my title, not A&E's) aired on June 2, 1995. There is an epilogue. Four years later I ran into Larry at Nate 'n' Al's Deli, his Beverly Hills hangout when visiting the West Coast. I reintroduced myself (to this day he's never told me if he saw the show) and buttonholed him about filmmaker Elia Kazan, who was about to be honored by the Academy of Motion Picture Arts and Sciences with a career Oscar® despite his disrepute for finking on his friends during the Blacklist era. "Why don't you do a show on it?" I asked. Larry shook his head and muttered, "No, it's not of general interest." I didn't have to make a counter argument because, within seconds, we were surrounded by other restaurant patrons who shared my position. Larry eventually did a show about the controversy.

While A&E was using "Shari Lewis & Lamb Chop" as an ass pillow, I persuaded them to let me do the story of Stan Lee. Hard to believe now that Marvel films have grossed billions of dollars, but Stan was a tough sell. In 1996 none of the Marvel characters that he had co-created had reached the screen in any noteworthy form; there had been a perfunctory *Captain America* movie and a *Fantastic Four* picture that, while interesting, was mired in legal limbo. Consequently, only comic book aficionados remembered who he was, and none of them worked for A&E. Stan's then-agent Don Kopaloff was also my agent at the time and he connected us. Once again everybody was cooperative, not only the Marvel people (who were in a corporate plummet that surfaced only after the show aired) but also Saban Entertainment, who owned many of the Marvel cartoon series. Remember, this was in the mid-1990s when the movie rights to Spider-Man® were tied in a cobweb, although James Cameron, who had agreed to make the movie, gave us a terrific but cautious interview about how he planned to shoot it. In addition to Cameron, we spoke to such diverse people as Gene Simmons of KISS (who said he learned English by reading Stan's writing), John Ritter, Lou Ferrigno (one of the most charismatic people I have ever met), Edward Asner, Chris Barnes, Mark Evanier, Harlan Ellison, John Buscema, John Romita, Terry Stewart, John Semper, Stan's brother Larry Lieber, Stan's wife Joanie, and their daughter J.C. (Sadly, Joan Lee passed away while this book was being edited.)

Screen Saver Too: *Hollywood Strikes Back*

The focus, of course, was Stan, who had told his story so any times that it should have been stale but, when he gave it his characteristic enthusiasm, never was. Then in his 70s, he is still—and as I write this he is in his 90s—the youngest kid in the room. As we conducted hours of interviews (the complete tapes are among my papers at UCLA) the through-line of the documentary emerged: no matter how famous Stan got, and no matter how great his influence was on popular culture, he felt he never achieved respect as a writer. Not just respect for himself, but for comic books as an art form. Even today, super-hero films are denigrated by calling them "comic book movies" when, in fact, comic books arguably represent a higher, more personal form of visual adventure. Some even consider them literature.

We taped Stan at his and Joanie's intricately decorated Hollywood Hills home, at his office at Marvel in West Los Angeles (he has long since left Marvel to form his own company, POW! Entertainment), and at San Diego Comic-Con. Although Comic-Con had been around since 1970, it only moved to the San Diego Convention Center in 1991 and had not yet become the mob scene it is today. Stan could walk the halls unnoticed and unbothered, and our "crew"—consisting of indefatigable producer Sue Nadell and me holding a mini-cam—had no trouble getting into any of the lightly attended events.

In designing the show, we tried to make the images, framing, and transitions look like comic art. This was before CGI and Paintbox became readily available, so our videographer Jake Clennell and his New York crew; and our LA crew Sovonto, Victor Smith, and Dasal Banks; hauled out all the tinted lights and gels. Then editors Mark Walters, Andy Corwin, and Alys Pitts added post-production bells and whistles. Everybody pulled in the same direction, so energized were we all, and we delivered it to the network with enthusiasm.

Then A&E sat on it.

Eventually "Stan Lee: The ComiX-Man" (their title, not mine) ran with "Shari Lewis & Lamb Chop" during a contrived "Childhood Heroes Week" (their title, not mine) between Christmas and New Year—traditionally the lowest television viewing period of the entire year. We never knew why.

The A&E experience became uncomfortable. They had become known as the Hitler Network because of all the World War Two documentaries they ran. By the time we had re-established the *Biography* brand they had acquired an even more disturbing moniker, "shows about dead white guys." Determined to prove this wrong, Sue Nadell and I compiled a list of African-Americans who we felt were worthy of profiling and submitted it to our network executive. The list included such luminaries as Crispus Attucks (the first casualty of the American Revolution), writer James Baldwin, inventor George Washington Carver, actress Cicely Tyson, and other black figures of similar stature.

All were rejected.

But that's not the most distressing part.

The person who had to tell us that all our black candidates were rejected was our network executive, who was black.

The *Biography* experience did have its lighter moments in a twisted sort of way. When co-host Peter Graves's seventieth birthday was nearing (he was born March 18, 1926), the A&E execs had the idea of throwing him a surprise party—on the air. The way to do this, they reasoned, was to have Graves's glib alternating host, the avuncular (sic) Jack Perkins, interrupt Graves during the taping of one of Graves's introductions to announce that "tonight's biography is about you, Peter." It was a genuinely sweet idea, but apparently it never occurred to these well-paid network honchos that Graves was bound to have caught on weeks earlier when we interviewed him for it. Although he was best-known as Jim Phelps in Bruce Geller's *Mission: Impossible* TV series from 1967-1973 and again in its revival from 1988-1990, Graves is best-loved for flying *Airplane!* in 1980 as Captain Clarence Oveur. He was also the younger brother of James Arness, the star of television's most popular (1955-1975) western series, *Gunsmoke* (the family name was Aurness). A&E was so keen to do the show that they said they had persuaded Arness, whose penchant for privacy was legendary, to be interviewed for it.

With that backstory I spent a delightful afternoon with Peter and his lovely wife Joan in their Pacific Palisades home in late January of 1996. The first thing I noticed was that they still had their Christmas tree up in the living room. A massive Scandinavian fur (Aurness is a Norwegian name), it looked like something on a season's greeting card. It also looked dangerously dry despite sitting in a pan of water. "The water keeps it moist," Peter assured me. "It's a tradition. We put it up on Christmas Eve and keep it up until Valentine's Day." The Graveses and I spent a pleasant hour or two—it was a secret pre-interview—and I left to report back to the network that Peter and Joan had been happily married for forty-six years, they were still wonderfully in love, he had been a Boy Scout, played the clarinet, and had been a working actor ever since moving from Minnesota to California in 1951. In other words, he was a very nice man and utterly normal. We would have to sweat to make him exciting. This is when they told me that we were supposed to play it as a practical joke. Without thinking, I blurted out, "You mean you're going to make fun of your own co-host?"

This is why I get fired a lot.

We didn't do the *Biography* of Peter Graves. Somebody else did. They did it straight. I didn't watch it. Why should I? I'd seen the play. In 2010, Peter died of a heart attack at the age of 84. He was a gentleman to the end. His life was one hell of a mission, and he chose to accept it.

At some point during this period I was asked by Twentieth Century-Fox to make the *Biography* of their co-founder, Darryl F. Zanuck. After I had been researching and writing the script for several weeks and had conducted a number of interviews, I became aware that the lines of authority at Fox Television were far different than those I was used to at Weller/Grossman. I foolishly thought that when I was hired to make a show, I'd be the one to make it. The reality was brought to my attention by my Fox executive who had been a good friend but turned out to be a bad manager. I discovered that, even though I was writing and producing, he would be directing. Rather than end a friendship, I ended my participation in the episode. I never saw the final results.

The A&E experience was both a privilege and a frustration. For the most part, it was remarkably hands-off and stimulating, but it ill-prepared me for the 27-year-old Jasons who would take over the industry within ten years and bring in the cancer of reality shows. They would also cut the budgets so that it is no longer possible in basic TV to make a living, let alone a killing.

Weller/Grossman Productions went out of business toward the end of the first decade of the 21st century, the victim of a change in FCC rules that allowed television networks—by now huge communications conglomerates—to once again produce and own the programs they aired rather than mandate that independent companies make them. Instantly thousands of people were put out of work, and all the channels began to look alike. Today six companies—which means six people—control ninety percent of what gets seen on the tube. The FCC and the Justice Department don't have a problem with this. After all, anyone can upload a video to YouTube and compete with Fox, Disney/ABC, Comcast/NBC, CNN/HBO/Time-Warner, Viacom, and CBS.

Screen Saver Too: *Hollywood Strikes Back*

Good Evenings

WHEN IT DEBUTED on San Francisco's Westinghouse-owned television station KPIX in August of 1976, *Evening Magazine* revolutionized the TV industry. It was not the first magazine show (that was arguably NBC's *Today* that bowed in 1952), but it was the first that took its viewers entirely out of doors and into the world. It also broke the broadcast networks' stranglehold on programming (Westinghouse/Group W was an independent web) and gave a career start to hundreds of people who would shape television for the next twenty years.

Evening was a heavily formatted half-hour series invented by Westinghouse programming executive Bill Hillier. A format is a menu with the sections of a show laid out in an orderly manner so the audience knows what to expect at every moment, yet within which there can be creativity (as long as the creativity isn't *too* creative). *Evening* featured two co-hosts (one of each) who talked viewers through three segments: the first and third ran six-and-a-half-minutes and were profiles of people and events. The middle segment was four 90-second lifestyle "tips" delivered by "tipsters" who were chosen for their lack of television experience. The overall tone of the show was upbeat to the threshold of fluff while remaining just serious enough so the occasional story would qualify as public affairs for purposes of meeting the stations' license commitment (see later). One story and one tip per episode had to be somewhat generic so that, even though the KPIX *Evening* was clearly shot in and around San Francisco, some of them could be shown in the other Group W markets in Boston (WBZ-TV), Baltimore (WJZ-TV), Pittsburgh (KDKA-

TV), and Philadelphia (KYW-TV). These were the pre-conglomerate days when owners were limited to five stations. The format allowed each station to construct a full half hour out of shared segments without having to shoot more than fifteen minutes.

Evening existed because of the Prime Time Access Rule, and the Prime Time Access Rule existed because of Group W President Donald McGannon. A former lawyer and executive with the Dumont television network, McGannon was made President of Group W in 1955. Although Westinghouse owned the television stations and held the broadcast licenses (they also had major radio holdings), they did not at that time produce their own programs. Instead, they were affiliated with one of the three existing networks, CBS, NBC, and ABC. Occasionally they would pre-empt network shows to air their own specials, not only when they disagreed with content but because McGannon bristled at the percentage of Group W's advertising revenue that the networks exacted as clearance fees. He figured that if local stations could hold onto at least one extra half hour per weekday they could not only increase their revenues but produce more local programming. To McGannon, both were important.

At that time the three networks produced four hours of prime time programming each day and demanded that their affiliates carry all of it. In the Eastern and Pacific time zones, this locked up schedules from 7 PM to 11 PM, and in the Central and Mountain time zones it was 6 PM to 10 PM. Starting in the 1960s, McGannon lobbied the FCC to cut back that bloc so that local stations could use the 7-8 PM hour (6-7 Central and Mountain) to run their own programming. In 1970 the Prime Time Access Rule was passed. Five years later, McGannon's Group W launched *Evening Magazine* to take advantage of the freed-up hour.

McGannon turned out to be idealistic. While he took the high road with the risky (at first) and expensive *Evening*, his local competitors chose to expand their profitable news or run syndicated game shows. With Hillier and a cadre of other creatives, he dove into the new ENG technology—Electronic News Gathering, a fancy name for portable three-quarter-inch videocassette cameras that would replace bulky 16mm sound cameras, whose film had to be laboriously processed after it was shot. Video was less cumbersome (despite needing fancier editing equipment[7]) and could go straight to air. He also took advantage of a jurisdictional battle between the company's two unions, the IATSE (studio cameras) and NABET (film cameras). While the IA and NABET were bickering over which would represent the new hybrid ENG technology, *Evening* went non-union.[8] This is another reason the show was shot outdoors; their young non-union crews were barred from using equipment inside the union building.

Evening Magazine's effect on television was immediate. Beneath the bright colors, sweet music, and chirpy manner of its on-air personalities, the show was a savvy (if cynical) distillation of what makes television work, although it's arguable whether it made television better. Producers were told to follow these rules:

1. Structure every story so you tell people what they're going to see, then show it to them, and then tell them what they've just seen;

2. People can absorb a piece of new information only every 30 seconds;

3. State old information in a new form so it will sound familiar. This instills feelings of comfort and superiority.

4. "Tips" should be single-idea stories structured using 1-3;

5. Always be promoting something: the next segment, the next show, the next fad. Give the appearance of being ahead of the curve (just not too far ahead.)

6. If you use subtlety, make it obvious.

It was easy to make fun of *Evening* and the press didn't miss a chance. The first shot they took was at its subtitle, *The MTWTF Show* (meaning Monday-Tuesday-Wednesday-Thursday-Friday). This may have looked good in the animated opening titles but it lent itself to being called, "The empty weeknight show" (say it out loud). The subtitle was quickly dropped.

In avoiding hard news and concentrating on "lifestyle" (which was a new word then), *Evening* offered a half-hour sigh of relief to a public that had been buffeted by Vietnam, Watergate, and national ennui. It drew in viewers by visiting neighborhoods all over the city, not because

---

7 A complete camera and editing system in the late 1970s could cost $250,000. Today the same thing (and more) can be done with an iPhone and a laptop.

8 This was not always the case—decisions were made on a station-by-station basis—but it goes to show intent.

there had been a car crash or tragedy there, but to boost local sights, people, and events. It was good for the community.

It was also good for Group W. Through a loophole in the FCC requirements that broadcasters serve their local markets, each station was able to get a full half-hour's credit toward their public service commitment by running only 15 minutes of actual public service programming. This explains why *Evening* was always searching for stories about charities, disabled people, municipal events, community leaders, and medical discoveries.[9]

San Francisco's *Evening* experiment proved so successful by the beginning of 1977 that Hillier made plans to open a franchise in Boston. By that time I had moved back to that city, having left my publicity career with Twentieth Century-Fox and United Artists in New York without a tear. This was when that great city hovered at the edge of bankruptcy—even the Manufacturers Hanover Trust couldn't afford to finish building their new bank on my street corner, if that's any indication of how bad things were. Naturally, New York's Democratic Mayor Abraham Beame asked Republican President Gerald Ford for financial help. Ford's refusal was characterized by *The Daily News* in its now-classic headline "Ford to City: Drop Dead."

Back in my beloved Massachusetts, with my publicity career happily behind me (see *Screen Saver*), I had sold a few articles to local newspapers and committed myself to being a journalist. In February of 1977, I was asked by Russ Manker, whom I had met through actor-singer Ted Neely (*Jesus Christ Superstar*), if I wanted to audition for *Evening*. Russ had been made Associate Producer of the incubating Boston show and he thought I might make a good "tipster" for their upcoming April launch. I arrived at the audition room (an office removed from the station) where Russ introduced me to Tom Ryder, the show's director, who pointed me to a desk. Instead of sitting behind it as I suspected they wanted, I sat on the edge. The cameraman had to tilt his camera up to accommodate me. Then they rolled tape and Tom asked me some

---

9 In 1985 the FCC, under Reagan appointee Marc Fowler, lifted the Fairness Doctrine, Equal Time doctrine, and the requirement that broadcasters serve their communities, giving them, in effect, perpetual licenses with no responsibility to benefit anybody except shareholders.

Screen Saver Too: *Hollywood Strikes Back*

questions. I answered them directly into the camera lens, ignoring him completely. I later learned that both of those decisions—choosing the edge of the desk and looking into the camera—were what landed me the job. In television, the less they have to teach you, the better.

I joined a cadre of tipsters who were notable in their professions. Maggie Lettvin was an exercise guru. Jim Wasco was a medical doctor. Nanci Glass was an expert on lifestyle. Ron Robin was one of Boston's top deejays, and so forth. Our team included studio producer Virginia Lyle (whom we called "VL"), cameramen/field producers Barry Rosenthal and Jim Arnold, and studio coordinator Maggie Hines. Other key show personnel were Melanie Chilek, Jonathan Tisch, Martin Doblmeier, Peter White, Paul Colardo, and Phillip Terrence. There were others who came and went, all of them fresh-faced, talented, and energetic. This must have been what TV was like in the early days. Practically everyone behind the camera, it seems, would go on to have a career beyond *Evening*, some of them substantial, and few of them even for Group W.

Ours would be the launch that would prove whether Hillier's franchise model worked. If it did, Baltimore, Pittsburgh, and Philadelphia would follow. The co-hosts of our show were Robin Young and Marty Sender, two sharp and ego-free personalities who were curious without being pushy and pleasant without being puerile. Marty was a seasoned newsman while still in his twenties, and Robin was a bright and empathetic interviewer. Our producer was Tom Houghton, a preppie-ish company man whose middlebrow taste assured this iteration of instant acceptance.

By design or default, *Evening* was not cutting-edge in content, only form. Its criteria for covering something was that somebody else had covered it first. The producers scoured dozens of magazines and newspapers to learn what was trending and then dispatched a crew to follow it. To this day I recall when Robin Young offered to arrange an interview with Robert De Niro, who had just co-starred with her brother, actor John Savage, in *The Deer Hunter*. De Niro never did interviews and this would have been a scoop, but, instead, she was told, "forget it; nobody's heard of him." (By this time he had won the Oscar for The *Godfather, Part II*.) I got the same turn-down for Richard Dreyfuss, whom I had known when I worked at United Artists in New York, and who would soon win the Oscar for *The Goodbye Girl*. He had also starred in *Jaws*, but apparently that wasn't enough to get him on *Evening Magazine*.

Hardly anybody else on the show had had any lengthy television experience, although the technicians and director (Bob Davis) who assembled each episode in the booth (once management reached an agreement with the union) did. But there was still a fertility dance over who got to touch what equipment. For example, as the show's movie tipster, I once carried a reel of 16mm film to Master Control to have it transferred to videotape. I made the mistake of setting it down on a table. When I tried to pick it up, I was informed that, if I didn't put it right back, the union would file a grievance against me, so I had to wait until an IATSE member could pick it up and bring it to the projector to thread. But wait, there's more. Once the transfer was finished, the film guy handed it back to me but we had to find a NABET film editor to rewind it and an IATSE member to hand me the videocassette we had just transferred it to. As a triple union man myself (SAG-AFTRA, Writers Guild, and IATSE, albeit a different local) I understood, and once I became accepted at the station, we were all able to joke about such rules (while scrupulously obeying them).

In the days before digital editing, *Evening* needed a one-month lead time between taping and airing, which meant that I often had to comment on a new film before having the chance to see it. Today, of course, it's all instantaneous, but the cumbersome post-production process in the late 1970s needed all the cushion it could get. For example, when *Star Wars* was due to open a month after I started, I had to tape my enthusiastic tip (not a real review) in April with only a press release and a color brochure to guide me. Only a week before the show aired did the astonishing film clips arrive from Twentieth Century-Fox and our editor frantically dropped them into the hole I'd left for them.[10]

I was encouraged to present my tips in costume. Why not? Anything to get attention. For *The Greatest*, a biography of Muhammad Ali in which Ali himself starred, I fought my way out of a huge paper bag on

---

10 Naturally I was at the theatre on opening day to see *Star Wars*. Of course, we ate it up, but I learned something important on the way out. The marquee read "Alec Guinness in *Star Wars*." They didn't get it. Neither the theatre nor the studio knew what they had or that audiences weren't coming to see Alec Guinness, they were coming to see *Star Wars*. How did audiences know what the business people did not? Answer that and you'll run Hollywood.

crowded Tremont Street in Beacon Hill. For *The First Nudie Musical* I appeared in Harvard Square wearing only a large barrel (like in the cartoons) to hide my lack of clothes. For *Sorcerer*, about men driving trucks laden with unstable nitroglycerine, I was tied to the back of a weaving flatbed and holding a goldfish bowl. For a movie about killer bees, *The Swarm*, I dressed up as a bee (shades of *Saturday Night Live*) and went from flower to flower in the Boston Public Garden as I delivered my spiel. For a segment on movie comedy teams I got pied by co-host Marty Sender and none other than Leonard Maltin a year before he rose to national prominence on *Entertainment Tonight*. Did someone say dignity?

Viewer complaints were a constant hazard; typically management supported strangers over their own people. After the pie incident, I got hate mail from viewers chastising me for wasting food (it was shaving cream). I should have been moved by their altruistic concern. Instead, I got a reprimand. In those days, the FCC required stations to keep viewer letters in a public file that could be inspected at license renewal time. I never heard of anyone ever asking to see the letters, and license renewals were usually rubber stamped, but, in preparing for them, the management had to leave the building and meet with community leaders to see how they could do a better job.

Like a wild cotton ball, if you pick through the fluff, you'll find seeds that mar the softness of the fiber. *Evening* was no different. When *The China Syndrome* was released in March 1979 it became a box office hit, in part, because it happened to hit theatres the same month as the partial meltdown at the Three Mile Island nuclear power station. (The film concerns a near-meltdown at a fictitious nuclear facility and the efforts of the owners of the nuke to silence the press.) Although Westinghouse manufactured equipment used in nuclear power plants, they were not involved in the disaster at Three Mile Island. Nevertheless, word came down from the "highest levels" that we were not to cover *The China Syndrome* in any way. When I later told this to the film's director, James Bridges, who was a friend, he passed word to the film's stars Jane Fonda and Jack Lemmon. None of them was surprised. I'm sure that my insistence on covering the film, which had become a mammoth box office hit, opened a file on me at Group W.

The next incident added to it. I believe I hold the record for viewer complaints over a segment I produced on Oscar-winning filmmaker

William Friedkin (whose biography, *Hurricane Billy*, I wrote in 1990). Friedkin was in Boston directing *The Brink's Job*. I had known him since doing local press for *The Exorcist* five years earlier, so when he came to Boston in the summer of 1978 to shoot the movie about the 1950 Brink's robbery, I had access to his set and the film's star Peter Falk. My interview with Friedkin had to, of course, include clips from his earlier films such as *The French Connection* and *The Exorcist*. At the time, no demonic possession scenes from *The Exorcist* had ever been broadcast. Friedkin and his assistant, Toni Lilly, secured permission for us to use one, which they cleared with Warner Bros. and everyone connected with it. In proud anticipation of my contacts and achievement, I sent memos all around *Evening* and WBZ advising them of these exclusive permissions. We edited the story and rolled it into the show. No big deal.

The moment I watched it at home, however, I knew we were in trouble. The scene we had used was the one in which Regan (Linda Blair) flops up and down on her bed, falls to the mattress, and her throat swells up to emit growls, followed by the demon's voice, "Keep away! The sow is mine!" It was strong stuff in the theatre (see earlier) and proved even stronger on TV. Had I known to do so, I would have applied what I call the "mother test." By this I mean that, before airing something, you need to ask yourself, "Would I be embarrassed if I was sitting next to my mother watching this?"

When the segment aired at 7:30 PM, the WBZ switchboard went crazy. Anybody who had seen *The Exorcist* when it came out in 1973 and had put it out of their minds suddenly had it all brought back in color at dinner time. Only my CYA ("Cover Your Ass") memos saved me from being fired right then and there, but it didn't help my future. I was reminded of Secretary of State Dean Acheson's sage maxim, "A memo is written not to inform the reader but to protect the writer." Ass-covering was the corporate rule at Group W, whose management style was somewhere to the right of the SS. They ruled by fear. Performance reviews were frequent and chilling. Employees were encouraged to attend station parties where there was an open bar, but the executives were always careful to drink ginger ale (which looked like scotch and soda) so they could stay sober while the workers got tipsy and talkative. The company was notorious for taking out blind "help wanted" ads in trade magazines so that, if any of their current employees blithely applied for the [non-existent] position in search of career advancement, he would be summoned to the personnel office and asked, "Aren't you happy here?" Such tactics produced a job atmosphere in which people were so paranoid that they had to stab each other in the front. Yet it also produced a solidarity among the studio crews that made them the best that I have ever had the privilege of working with, no doubt because certain management could be such dicks.

I had been freelancing for *Evening* for two years, turning out one tip a week and moving into producing longer stories, something no other tipster was allowed to do. The people were fun and the insanity had by this time settled down to a smoothly running show. Sometimes my work was even picked up in Baltimore, Pittsburgh, and Philadelphia, who, by now, had their own successful *Evenings*. In November 1979, I was looking forward to the holidays and walking through Harvard Square when I happened to see my camera crew set up in a housewares store on JFK Street. They were taping a cooking segment with Dave Maynard, a mainstay of WBZ radio whose *Community Auditions* was a beloved Boston tradition. Dave's tips often preceded mine on *Evening* and, at the end of his 90-second monologues, he always threw it to me with, "Now let's see what Nat Segaloff is up to in the *Evening* Leisure Department." I marveled at Dave's ability to ad lib for 90 seconds without having to cut, but I squirmed as he passed 90 seconds and headed toward two minutes. When he finished I asked him why he went long. Was it for the holidays? No, he told me warily; hadn't I heard?

"Heard what?" I said.

He was direct: "Nat, they took you off the show."

I hurried to the station where I found Tom Houghton at his desk. We chatted for a few minutes as I gave him, I thought, a fair chance to bring up the elephant in the room. When he didn't, I said, "Is there anything you need to tell me?"

"No, I can't think of anything," he said.

"I just bumped into Dave Maynard and I thought there was something I should know about me and the show."

"Oh, that's right," Tom suddenly remembered. "We're not using you any more."

Thanks to Dave, I wasn't shocked. I wasn't even angry. "Is there any particular reason?"

"They took a survey in Ohio and it was determined that we have too many mustachioed Jewish males."

"You mean you showed my tapes to an audience that wasn't from Boston and didn't know me?"

"Uh-huh."

I shook my head in bewilderment. "I don't suppose you want to show me the survey, do you?"

"No I don't."

And that was that. Shortly after, *Evening Magazine* franchised itself nationally, changing its name to *PM Magazine* and licensing its format, graphics, and music to one station per market for $1,000 a week. The *PM* stations could use as many or as few existing segments from the national reel as they wished. Soon Group W was collecting upwards of $100,000 a week for just dubbing tapes. It was brilliant. (Strangely, it never bothered Westinghouse that their money-making *PM* had the same name as a Left-wing Chicago newspaper of the 1940s.) I later briefly worked for the Providence, Rhode Island and Hartford, Connecticut *PM*s which went smoothly and pleasantly. I guess they didn't know anybody in Ohio.

Evening ended in whatever forms it existed in 1991. In 1996, the Prime Time Access Rule was rescinded by Bill Clinton's FCC under Chairman Reed Hundt. Don McGannon did not live to see his work destroyed by politics and lobbying; he had died in 1984 after a losing battle with Alzheimer's Disease. Celebrating him at a memorial service, one of his successors spoke eloquently of his achievements and ended by saying, "Toward the end of his life, Don could not remember any of us. But tonight, we remember Don."

Astonishingly, I had a revival at WBZ in the early 1980s through the intervention of Linda Harris, a former *Evening* tipster whose elegance and intelligence had landed her a morning show, *4 Today* (WBZ was channel 4), broadcast live from the studio. She asked me to be her film critic, which involved getting up at 4 AM to make it to the station by 5 AM, write my copy to teleprompter, and be in my on-set desk at 6:40 AM. The hours were hell but the crews, as I wrote earlier, were superb and every day was a party. When the gig ended—I knew it was only for a short time because WBZ was looking for a full-time film critic[11] and it wouldn't be me (because I was a mustachioed Jewish male)—I was allowed to say goodbye on the air, live. Or so I thought. Only after we signed off did they tell me that management had put me on seven-second delay in case I said something bad about them. This was insulting but not surprising. Instead of sulking, I moved over to WSBK-TV, a UHF super-station, and joined a show called *Movie Loft & Company*, hosted by Dana Hersey, perhaps the most skilled on-air person I have ever worked opposite.

Meanwhile my experience was tapped when I was asked to become the television columnist for *The Real Paper*, a feisty alternative weekly published in Cambridge, Massachusetts. My editor was Monica Collins, a take-no-prisoners reporter who inspired fear in those who needed to be afraid and devotion from those of us who respected her. Shortly after I started I was invited to WBZ to see some of their new shows and was met in the hallway by Dick Kurlander, the Program Manager with whom I had had several run-ins while working under him.

"Congratulations on the *Real Paper* column," he said. "I hope you'll give us a fair shake."

"You've got nothing to worry about, Dick," I said, chipping him playfully on his shoulder. "I promise that if I can't say something nice, I won't say anything at all."

I kept my promise. I never wrote a bad word about WBZ. In fact, I never wrote about them at all.

---

11 They hired Joyce Kulhawik, a former *Evening* tipster, who served nearly thirty years and tirelessly covered Boston's creative community. We're still friends.

Little Stick-Up at Brink's

AFTER TONY PINO and his gang of North End misfits robbed the Brink's garage of $2.775 million on January 17, 1950 it took the FBI six years and $29 million to learn what everybody in the neighborhood had known all along. Noel Behn wrote about it in his 1971 book *Big Stick-Up at Brink's*, and in 1976 producer Dino De Laurentiis started turning it into a movie to be directed by John Frankenheimer. When Frankenheimer rejected the script by George V. Higgins (*The Friends of Eddie Coyle*), he dropped out and William Friedkin was brought in. This is a prime example of the Hollywood carousel: Frankenheimer had directed the unnecessary 1975 sequel to Friedkin's 1971 *The French Connection* (*French Connection II*), and Friedkin, smarting from the failure of *Sorcerer* (1977), signed on to replace Frankenheimer. Although Friedkin facetiously said that he agreed to make the picture because it was set in Boston and it would allow him to see his beloved Boston Celtics play basketball, he also said yes because he had just failed to get financing for *Born on the Fourth of July* despite having Al Pacino (*The Godfather* and *The Godfather, Part II*) in the lead.

With a new screenplay by Walon Green (*The Wild Bunch*), Friedkin shot *The Brink's Job* in Boston in the summer of 1978. De Laurentiis's line producer, Ralph Serpe, made overall arrangements, but Friedkin was supported by such trusted associates as former New York City detectives Sonny Grosso and Randy Jurgensen, casting director Lou DiGiaimo, editor Bud Smith, and prop master Barry Bedig.

Screen Saver Too: *Hollywood Strikes Back*

I was overjoyed at being able to hang out with Billy, whom I had come to know in the wake of *The Exorcist* and with whom I had stayed in touch, particularly after the financial debacle of *Sorcerer*, which I reviewed on *Evening Magazine* and called the greatest American film since *Citizen Kane*. Perhaps my excitement overcame my perspective, but I still hold *Sorcerer* to be a mammoth cinematic achievement, easily in the top 100, and am proud to have said so at the time of its release when so many others (including Friedkin) were doubters. At least, I figured, I could get our *Evening Magazine* cameras onto the closed *Brink's* set.

"I don't know," said Friedkin's assistant, Toni Lilly. "Billy just kicked Paramount's behind-the-scenes crew off the set a couple of days ago." Later she called back and said, "Billy says he'd love to have you." A date was set and a deal was struck—not with Friedkin, but with *Evening Magazine*(q.v.), who wouldn't let me profile the director unless I also shot a story on the film's star, Peter Falk, whom we were told was not interested in doing interviews. Once again, Billy intervened and we were on.

In addition to Falk, the cast included some of the finest actors in the business: Paul Sorvino, Warren Oates, Allen Gorwitz (formerly Allen Garfield, then Allen Gorwitz, then back to Garfield), Peter Boyle, Gena Rowlands, and relative newcomers Kevin O'Connor and Gerald Murphy. The sets were designed by Dean Tavoularis (of Lowell, Massachusetts), who had just turned 1974 New York into 1917 for *The Godfather, Part II* and was about to make the Philippines look like Vietnam for *Apocalypse Now*. The assistant directing team included my old friends Terry Donnelly, Jonathan Sanger, and Mark Johnson (later to win the Oscar for producing *Rainman*). Talk about access.

Our *Evening* crew—Robin Young, Jim Arnold, and Sid Levin—spent a long and hot (it was a Boston summer) day at 600 Commercial Street, the former Brink's garage which had been restored to its Fifties condition. The sequence we covered (that never made it into the finished film) involved Tony Pino leading his ragtag gang into the Brink's offices, which were routinely kept unlocked, and crawling along on the floor to avoid being recognized by guards that weren't there. In fact, that was Brink's dark secret: the company had no security. They found it cheaper to pay stolen losses out of their profits than to hire guards and install good locks. They existed on reputation, not reality—until the night of January 17, 1950, that is.

It was while we were editing our story and the *Brink's* people were editing theirs that the real fun started.

In order to be able to turn Boston's 1978 Italian North End into 1950, location manager Carmine Foresta and producer Ralph Serpe had to negotiate with each resident of the streets where filming would take place to move their modern cars, remove their window air conditioners and take down their television aerials, none of which were there when the Brink's robbery happened. Once word got around that the film company was paying people to take down television antennas, the next day every apartment in the North End sported a brand new television antenna.

That may have been folksy, but on Friday, July 28, 1978 it got serious. There was a knock on the door of Bud Smith's editing room at 441 Stuart Street. Smith was out at the time, but his son, Scott, was there as three masked gunman pushed their way in, hit him on the side of the head, and bound and gagged everyone on the editorial crew but one, whom they forced, at gunpoint, to screen footage for them. When they were finished they made off with thirteen reels of cut footage, primarily crowd scenes, which they knew would cost a fortune to reshoot.

On learning of the robbery, Friedkin's first concern was whether anyone had been hurt. Then he laughed; the footage that had been taken was workprint, a rough copy of the film used for editing; the original negative was safely stored in the lab in California. When the expected extortion call came in later from the bandits demanding $300,000 for return of the footage, the FBI had instructed Friedkin to offer them $20,000 and not to leak that the footage had already been replaced. Instead, Friedkin told them, "Go rent a projector and enjoy yourselves," and hung up.

How does *Evening Magazine* fit into this? I happened to be in the Brink's production offices talking to Toni when the robbery took place down the hall. The Boston Police immediately shut down the premises and wouldn't let me out. Worse, they wouldn't let me use the phone to call WBZ to tell the News Director that I was not only *on* the scene of the crime, I was *in* the scene of the crime (this was before cell phones). Moreover, having made films myself, I knew right away that the thieves had only taken worthless workprint, as anyone in WBZ's NABET would agree.

Screen Saver Too: *Hollywood Strikes Back*

An hour later I was released and I immediately took a cab to the station, telling the News Director, "We have exclusive inside footage of the cast and crew of Brink's."

"Really?" he said. "Where did you get it?"

"We shot it for *Evening* Magazine."

His voice sank. "I'm sorry," he said. "We can't use it."

"Why not?"

"Because *Evening* is non-union and we can't air non-union footage even if our own station shot it." This is how corporate news works.

No one ever found out who robbed Bud Smith's editorial suite, but on December 14, 1978—a week after the film was released—the story broke from NBC investigative reporter Brian Ross that Dino De Laurentiis was claiming that the film ran $1 million over budget because of shakedowns by Boston's Teamsters and certain organized crime figures. The next day Friedkin flew to Boston and held a press conference. He swore no knowledge of the payoffs (he was too busy making the movie) and stated that, while he occasionally employed people who had been in jail, he "was not aware that it was against the law in this country to hire a worker with a criminal record." He later told me in an interview which I aired on CBS's WEEI-FM that he found some criminals to be more honorable than some policemen. This drew a call from the FBI asking me for a copy of the interview which, because it had aired, I had neither right nor reason to withhold.

In 1981, four men were ultimately indicted for racketeering, mail fraud, and extortion on five Boston-based productions between 1977 and 1979, one of them *The Brink's Job*.[12] The charges were against Teamster organizer and trustee Joseph "Gus" Manning and drivers William C. Bratton, Hartley E. Greenleaf, and Ernest C. Sheehan. On February 5, 1982 Bratton and Greenleaf were found guilty and on March 8 were sentenced. Bratton was handed two years for racketeering and three years (suspended) for mail fraud; Greenleaf got two years for racketeering and two (suspended) for mail fraud. Manning and Sheehan did not withstand trial; Manning suffered a heart attack during the proceedings and Sheehan had cancer. Boston's Teamsters have worked ever since to cleanse their reputation and attract film production to Massachusetts.

---

12 The others were *Oliver's Story, International Velvet, James at 15,* and *See How She Runs*.

The Brink's Job grossed in the neighborhood of $8 million on a $12 million budget (including, apparently, the $1 million paid to the Mob). It's an agreeably goofy picture—De Laurentiis and Friedkin wanted it to be about a bunch of screw-ups ala *Big Deal on Madonna Street* (Mario Monicelli, 1958)—but it didn't stand a chance in the solar storm of escapist science fiction following *Star Wars* the year before (*Close Encounters of the Third Kind, Alien, Invasion of the Body Snatchers, Superman, Battlestar Galactica,* etc.). But I shall always remember it as the film that held me hostage and solidified my disillusionment about the TV news business. And they never did find the stolen footage.

Screen Saver Too: *Hollywood Strikes Back*

Strange Interludes

PUBLICITY INTERVIEWS are an implied agreement between the reporter asking the questions and the celebrity answering them. Consensual and arranged by a public relations representative, they carry the expectation that a positive article will come out of the encounter. Neither side expects that an earthshaking revelation will emerge, but the celebrity depends on the exposure to sell his product and the reporter counts on the celebrity's fame to draw an audience.

Described in such a perfunctory—if not a mercenary—manner, it seems cut-and-dried. Yet the news industry thrives on interviews and the promise of what they might, just might, reveal. A skilled reporter can dig beneath the surface while a skilled celebrity can see that he doesn't. The promise and the tease are why they can be so fascinating.

I lost count years ago of how many interviews I've conducted, although I saved the audiocassettes for most of them, not so much for the archive I hoped to someday open as to cover my butt in case anyone claimed I'd misquoted them. The length of an interview is half an hour, or one cassette side, but I may have used only six minutes of it on the air or ten sentences in print. The rest is either off-subject or connective material. Nevertheless, some people stand out, either because their film did too, or because they were so interesting.

Like Richard Attenborough. Long before he was knighted, everybody called him "Dickie," and he was in good form while plugging his 1985 film *A Chorus Line*. The film was a disappointment (most people said that the first twenty minutes of Bob Fosse's 1979 *All That Jazz* did it first and did it better), but Attenborough wasn't. Upbeat and engaging, he still smarted from early career rejection as an actor, even though, as a director, he received the 1982 Oscar for *Gandhi* (which also won the Oscar for Best Picture, even against *E.T. The Extraterrestrial*). Like all actors, he remembers his first major review as a performer, and it was dismal. "It was a movie of a Graham Greene novel called *Brighton Rock*," he could now smile, "and there was a reviewer and his name was—I can tell you everything about him—his name was Leonard Mosely and he wrote for the London *Daily Express*. 'Pinky Brown' was the little seventeen-year-old gangster I played. And Leonard Mosely said, 'Richard Attenborough's Pinky is as close to Graham Greene's original as Greta Garbo is to Donald Duck.' Now, you can't top that, can you?" It's hard panning a film made by someone you like, and *A Chorus Line*'s publicists counted on it.

On the other hand, there's nothing as joyous as a press junket for a film that everybody loves. That was what we enjoyed for *Ghost* (1990) when Demi Moore, Patrick Swayze, and Tony Goldwyn met a friendly, if not giddy, press corps. The one who seemed most at ease was Whoopi Goldberg, who would win an Oscar as the fake psychic who turns out to be a real one. One of *Ghost*'s most moving moments happens when Goldberg channels Swayze so he can give Moore an intimate goodbye. Someone asked her why director Jerry Zucker replaced her with "Bud" Swayze when the two started kissing. "Are you kidding?" Goldberg said, "I just got over *The Color Purple*!"

When comedian Howie Mandel became a television mainstay in 2005 as host of television's *Deal or No Deal*, he was coming full circle. He started off as a carpet salesman in Canada.[13] "I once got fined," he recalled at the time of his 1986 film, *A Fine Mess*, which unfortunately lived up to its name at the box office. "This couple wanted cheaper and cheaper and cheaper and I didn't have anything cheaper, so finally I just showed 'em the rubber underpadding. I said, 'This is new rubberized carpet; look how it wears,' and I poured my Pepsi on it and I wiped it up, and they said, 'Oh, that really wears good,' and I sold it. For living room, dining room, three bedrooms, and a hall: rubber underpadding. I was so

---

13 Sidebar: Groucho Marx said that if you want a reporter to get a joke right, you have to tell it to him wrong. Not always. Notice how Howie Mandel words these three anecdotes so they make sense when presented verbatim. He knows how to structure a story and keep it lean. This is why comedians often make good actors but actors seldom make good comedians.

Screen Saver Too: *Hollywood Strikes Back*

excited I told all my friends. And about three weeks later they called me back complaining that they were vacuuming their living room and a piece of the carpet came up. I got nervous and said, 'Listen, you don't *vacuum* rubber carpet.' She said, 'But it's dirty, what do you do?' I said, 'You *erase* it.' She called the Better Business Bureau and they fined me $500 and made me put carpet in."

Howie also had the rights to import a toy flasher doll. "It had a trench coat and you'd open it up and see"—he smiles playfully—"that it was physically correct. What happened was, they wouldn't allow it past the border. When I got the rights, I shipped a gross of them [from the USA] and they said they were pornographic and they wouldn't let them into Canada. It was a novelty item, and in order to get them in, I had to ship the dolls and then ship the parts separately. The dolls got in, and then I had to go to Customs and claim the crate of 'parts.' They were made out of cotton. And the guys at Customs, they were picking them up and going, 'What are these? What are you gonna use 'em for?' And I was laughing. They never let me take 'em, and that business never really got off the ground. Somewhere in U.S. Customs in Detroit there's a crate of 144 cotton genitals."

Unsurprisingly, Mandel was always funny—except in school where, as he says, "I was in trouble. I was asked to leave school (he attended three different high schools) and didn't know that what I did would translate into a job until [the TV comedy game show] *Make Me Laugh*. My friends always enjoyed it, but I was barred from every restaurant, every mall. One time this woman was standing between me and another table and I was eating and she was bending over talking to somebody else and her rear end was right at my table for, like, twenty minutes. So I took the fire extinguisher off the wall and put it under the table and I aimed the hose. She was wearing a dress and I shot the foam up the dress. So they asked me to leave. Can you believe that?"

On a more serious note, Martin Ritt—a good friend and a great director (*Hud, Norma Rae, Sounder*)—took time away from his press tour for the eminently likable *Murphy's Romance* (1985) to talk privately about his filmmaking technique. (This is where being a critic with a film school degree comes in handy.) In his time, Marty worked with three of the greatest directors of photography the movies have ever known: James Wong Howe, John Alonzo, and William Fraker. Although Ritt always felt that "the style is the perfect extension of the content of the film," he surprised me by revealing that the DP sometimes dictated the style of the acting.

"Alonzo, because he works with the hand-held Panaflex all the time, gives the film a different rhythm," he explained. "I'm aware of that and therefore the scenes are staged in a certain way and acted in a certain way so that the rhythm will be in keeping with what is being played. With Fraker, who is really much more of a classicist, I'm prepared to sit and wait and do things differently. Jimmy Wong Howe, who was really an incredible artist, had both elements in him. He was a funny guy; that's true of many cameramen. I've not really said this, Nat, because I don't want to hurt anybody's feelings unnecessarily—on important subjects I will—most of 'em can't read a script. They don't know. At the end of two weeks of shooting *Hud*, Jimmy came to me one day and said, 'Now I know what you mean. Now I understand what you said to me at the beginning of this picture.' I had said, 'Jim, we need infinity in this picture. Everything should be backlit.' We have high plains in West Texas. They should be never-ending. There's a kind of respect, reverence for landscape."[14]

Because of tight budgets, it is unusual for directors to get rehearsal time with actors prior to production and even rarer for directors of photography to attend them. "I invited Fraker to rehearsals on [*Murphy's Romance*]," Ritt said. "He went bananas. He'd never been to a rehearsal of any kind in his life. He'd been working in pictures where you show up, you line it up, you shoot it."

Rehearsals are important not only so the actors can get a handle on their characters but so the director can get a handle on the actors. If they're not working out, it's better to replace them before shooting starts. Sometimes, however, a performance has to be constructed in the editing room if it isn't there on the set. "It's possible if you have that in mind when you're shooting the film," Ritt said in his gruff but sensitive voice. "If you knew there were certain things that the actor couldn't do consistently and you found enough in each take to, in your mind's eye, put it together, it's possible to make an ordinary actor pretty good. I've done

---

14 *Hud* won Howe the Academy Award® for Best Cinematography, Black and White in 1964. When he and Ritt made *Hombre* four years later, their first film together in color, Ritt joked that Howe had to look on the box of Kodak to learn how to shoot it. In fact, Howe had been one of the pioneers of Technicolor starting with *Tom Sawyer* (1938).

that in editing where he was so busy, he had so many bad habits, that he wouldn't stop. I cut them all out of the performance when I started to put the film together. But it's not a good way to go."

Ritt made only two films after *Murphy's Romance*: *Nuts*, starring Barbra Streisand and Richard Dreyfuss, and *Stanley & Iris*, with Jane Fonda and Robert De Niro. Before those, however, he took some time off to teach at UCLA, "Because nobody that's teaching in a university today is prepared to say the things that I'm going to say to those kids. I ran some of my films at UCLA last year and I was surprised to find out how conservative the kids were. If I can take six of their graduate students and help them produce their scripts, I can do a service to that school and for those kids. And I'm gonna do it."

"That means you'll have to grade papers, too," I said, as I closed my note pad.

"I don't think so," Marty grinned. "It'll be dailies."

Although Ritt often drew fire for being politically progressive, in his entire career he made only two overtly political films: *The Molly Maguires* (1970) about the 1876 mineworkers' revolt in Pennsylvania, and *The Front* (1976) about the Blacklist. His other films were about the human condition: literacy, racism, sexism, and just plain survival. Marty was a survivor, too: of the Blacklist, of the studios, and of a growing superficiality in American culture. "It's a time that Dalton Trumbo called, in the fifties, 'The time of the toad,'" he told me in the mid-80s. "It's gotta swing back. It's got to." Marty died in 1990 at the age of 76, still waiting.

Private print interviews like this are a privilege. They are usually given to interviewers whose publications are important or because the filmmaker and reporter have a personal relationship. Then there's eyewash. Eyewash is a fake interview. It happens when a publicist faces an indifferent press and has trouble filling up a celebrity's schedule. In order to avoid embarrassment, the publicist will ask a trusted reporter to interview the client even if there is no promise that the results will ever run. I have been known to do this as a courtesy, sometimes in exchange for a meal at a good restaurant, at other times in expectation of a return favor down the line, and sometimes just out of friendship.

Then there are the "none of the above" interviews. I was asked by the Orson Welles Cinema in Cambridge, Massachusetts to interview Craig Russell, the star of their cult hit *Outrageous!* Russell played a female impersonator who shares a flat with an emotionally troubled woman, Hollis McLaren. The film's melodrama took a back seat to Russell's fabulous—and I mean FABulous—impressions of Bette Davis, Mae West, Carol Channing, and other gay icons. When I sat beside him on a love seat and turned on my tape recorder, I told him that—seeing him in street clothes (except for the eye makeup)—he reminded me of Ida Lupino. This not only broke the ice, it melted it. For the next twenty minutes he played to an audience that wasn't there (it was the Welles Cinema's upstairs office) and it was immediately clear that he was not fueled merely by the excitement of our interview but by a substance I couldn't place and he couldn't buck. He died in 1990 after making a sequel (*Too Outrageous!*) and a few other films, but mostly toured the gay club circuit. To this day I'm not sure whether my interview was with him or Ida Lupino.

Peter Cushing was strange in another way. I was asked to interview him by Patty Ecker of Cinerama Releasing Corporation, the distributor that had picked up his latest British horror film, *The House That Dripped Blood* (1972). A soft-spoken, frail-looking man with sunken cheeks and a shock of thinning white hair combed straight back, he was, in person, far from the mad scientists, vampire hunters, and detectives that he had built a career playing in a succession of Hammer and Rosenberg/Subotsky horror films. (He would ascend into immortality in 1977 when he portrayed Grand Moff Tarkin in the original *Star Wars* and have an apotheosis when he was digitally resurrected in *Rogue One: A Star Wars Story* in 2016.)

"The main problem I have with the scripts I'm given," he said in his posh accent, "is that they have extra words." *The House That Dripped Blood* was written by Robert Bloch, author of *Psycho*, but I let his criticism pass. "They're always adding phrases like, 'Well' or "you know' to dialogue as if one character needs to get the other's attention. Screenwriters try to make dialogue sound like people talk. That isn't what cinema should be. Cinema is not actual reality, it has its own reality."

While Cushing spoke, he slipped a single white glove onto his left hand, placed a cigarette in a holder, and carefully lit it. He inhaled far more deeply than I thought such a slight man could manage, then let the smoke out with what sounded like a long, forlorn sigh. "I miss my wife," he said, apropos of nothing. (Mrs. Cushing—Violet Helene Beck—had died in January 1971 and this was February 1972). "I miss her every day. I can't wait until I die so I can join her."

Cushing finally got his wish on August 11, 1994 at the age of 81. Five years earlier he had been made Officer of the Order of the British Empire for his services to British theatre. I have no record of having used the interview—I didn't want my readers and listeners slashing their wrists—but I was strangely moved to have shared time with a man who faced death so often on the screen that he yearned to meet it in person.

Butterfly McQueen was another remarkable personality whose interview required discretion. I was invited by my friend Ken Rogoff to a small dinner party at the South End Boston home of musician, activist, and chef Maddie Mangan (whose jambalaya recipe I still use). On arrival, I was surprised that the guest of honor was the actress who had memorably played Prissy, the addled house servant, in *Gone with the Wind*. I was also surprised that, in real life, Miss McQueen sounded just like Prissy, albeit more soft-spoken and, of course, far more intelligent. Aware of nutrition and food additives, McQueen swore that she could taste the aluminum lining on the tin of crushed pineapple that Maddie mixed into her cornbread (I still use that recipe, too).

Where this was a social occasion not connected with movie publicity, I formally asked Miss McQueen if we might speak on the record for a few moments for my newspaper. She consented and, of course, the subject became *GWTW*. We both acknowledged the film's troubling positive portrayal of slavery, but I was surprised when she recounted how she had resisted the stereotyping of black performers and that her stance had caused her to be considered "difficult" in Hollywood. She also insisted that her co-star, Hattie McDaniel, had likewise suffered because she resisted playing stereotypes (in fact, McDaniel had a far more successful career than McQueen). What I wasn't prepared for was her next comment: that all the black people in America should move back to Africa because they'd be happier there. I wanted to pursue this conversation to see if McQueen was a follower of Marcus Garvey, but I also knew I could never put it into my story lest it reinforce the racism that festered in certain parts of my *Boston Herald* newsroom. Fortunately, Miss McQueen came to her own rescue. "Now then, Mr. Segaloff," she said quietly yet firmly, "I think we've had enough time to talk. Let's prepare for dinner."

Tragically, McQueen died in 1995 when a fire broke out in her home near Augusta, Georgia where she had been living anonymously—the same Georgia that had refused to allow her to attend the 1939 premiere of *Gone with the Wind* because Loew's Grand was a white-only theatre. Thelma Butterfly McQueen was no fool, even though she often portrayed them, and I wish I had known more of her history when I found myself shaking her hand on that unexpected encounter. She was, I later learned, a member of the Freedom from Religion Society and said, in their support, "As my ancestors are free from slavery, I am free from the slavery of religion." Fiddle-Dee-Dee indeed.

Screen Saver Too: *Hollywood Strikes Back*

Magic Time

ACCORDING TO OBSERVERS, before he began every take of each film he made, Jack Lemmon would take a breath, close his eyes, and say to himself, "Magic time." This was his way of preparing to lift the words off the page and give them life. Similarly, Orson Welles, who studied magic, used to say that a film director is a man who presides over accidents. What both men were saying is that motion pictures are an alchemy of craft, talent, and luck. This chapter is about craft—not just craft, but craft that creates magic for the audience.

Everybody thinks he wants to see the secret behind magic tricks, but magicians know better; an illusion explained is a dream shattered. Nevertheless, Hollywood and live theatre often give away their creative secrets as a way of attracting audiences. That's why the the public craves learning how certain films are made and how stage effects are produced, even if it spoils the illusion. Or they think they do. As Blanche DuBois says in *A Streetcar Named Desire*, "I don't want realism. I want magic! Yes, yes, magic! I try to give that to people. I misrepresent things to them. I don't tell the truth, I tell what ought to be the truth. And it that's sinful, then let me be damned for it!"

The cleverest revelations about movies are those that tell just enough to make you want to see the film. One of the most remarkable men in this tantalizing field was Jimmy MacDonald, the premiere sound effects man for the Walt Disney Studios from 1934 to his retirement in 1986. It was Jimmy whose inventiveness created the sounds for Disney animation and occasional live-action films in the era before such things could be digitally generated or, indeed, before portable sound recording equipment made it possible to capture real effects and bring them into the studio. He also took over voicing Mickey Mouse in 1946 when Walt, who did him from "Steamboat Willie" (1928) on, became too busy.

Jimmy began as a drummer, something that early sound effects men had in common because of drummers' precise timing and the ability to play a range of percussion equipment. In those days cartoons were post-synced, which involved showing them on a screen and recording everything—voices, music, effects—live.

Every couple of years, the Disney PR people would show off MacDonald to the press. It was like inviting kids to a magic show. Jimmy demonstrated how he made the sound of raging wind (a wheel that scraped against loose fabric); rain (small nails inside a ribbed drum); a bear's growls (he growled into the globe of a hurricane lamp); the screeching sound of a locomotive stopping (diamond cutting pane glass); and the venerable sound of horses' hooves (coconut shells). But the most remarkable effect was the one he'd devised for *The Love Bug* (1968). It was effect for a wheel popping off an axle, rolling down a hill, spinning on the ground, and settling. For this, Macdonald dropped a BB in a balloon, blew it up, and twirled the balloon so that centripetal force made the BB spin around inside. He held it against a microphone and there was the whir (*voom-voom-voom*), then it slowed down in pitch (*vuum-vuum-vuum*), then it dropped to the bottom and bounced (*bop-bop-bopbopbop*). Then we applauded.[15]

The Disney people loved giving away their secrets, but only on their TV shows and only for special effects ("The Plausible Impossible," "Tricks of Our Trade," etc.) Try getting them to reveal their budgets or grosses for a newspaper article and you might as well ask the White House for the nuclear codes.

Sound effects are always a source of wonder. Decades ago, National Public Radio spoke to Ben Burtt about his audio design for *Star Wars* when he told of hearing the sound of a laser bolt being fired outside his office window. It was a pneumatic jackhammer that was misfiring at a construction site, so he ran out and recorded it. The NPR commentator

---

15 Attempting a written description is lunacy but you can do this at home with a balloon and a BB and you'll hear what I mean.

Screen Saver Too: *Hollywood Strikes Back*

summarized by saying, "What kind of a person would know what a laser bolt would sound like?"

Most people are aware of how to make basic sound effects: crinkling cellophane sounds like fire; shaking a sheet of metal creates thunder; twisting a leather wallet sounds like squeaky shoes; and pulling a sheet of paper out of a manila envelope is what the automatic doors sound like on the U.S.S. *Enterprise*. But wait, there's more.

One afternoon several years ago I was at a spotting session for a movie when sound designer Paul Huntsman played me the effect of someone being stabbed. Obviously they didn't really plunge a knife into anyone.

"What did you use?" I asked.

"A chicken," Paul said. He meant a supermarket chicken.

"Why a chicken?"

"Because rib roast was $4.49 a pound."

Nowadays, even though it's possible to digitally fabricate or alter most any audio effect, it's easier to use Foley.[16] The process is named after Jack Donovan Foley who perfected it while working at Universal Pictures, which he did until 1967. It's an outgrowth of radio sound effects where footsteps, doors, clothing rustling, and other noises are recorded in real time against the projected film (just like Disney did with "Steamboat Willie" forty years earlier). Foley artists must match their footsteps to that of the actors, and they trod on a number of different surfaces (wood, tile, cement, gravel, etc.) as they work. They also clink drinking glasses, ruffle clothing, open and close doors, and make other post-synchronized sounds. I had the pleasure of collaborating with Robin Harlan for our live broadcast/simulcast of *The First Men in the Moon* that Alien Voices did for the Sci-Fi Channel in 1997. As the scriptwriter adapting H. G. Wells' novel, I challenged Robin and her team to produce the sound of pre-chewed food being fed to someone, opening and closing space capsules, trudging through snow, and other imaginary effects. She was undaunted. The squishy sound of food was produced by a child's squeeze toy half-filled with water; the space capsule doors were heavy pieces of metal scraped against each other; and the crunch of footsteps on snow (this one amazed me) was produced by squeezing a box of corn starch.

---

16 Ironic tangent: Years ago I helped a friend move into a new apartment. The whole time, the people upstairs kept walking back and forth. We went upstairs to see if there was a problem. The name on their door was "Foley."

There are showbiz secrets other than sound effects. Director of Photography Oswald Morris famously said that he got the misty, nostalgic look of Norman Jewison's film of *Fiddler on the Roof* by stretching a nylon stocking across the camera's matte box. *Star Wars* effects master Richard Edlund made the Millennium Falcon shoot into hyper space by doing a simple zoom shot on a photograph of stars. Special effects people have known for years that Hershey's chocolate syrup looks like blood in black and white films (such as *Psycho*). You don't need to be a magician, you just need to remember that cinema, as Martin Scorsese says, "is a matter of what's in the frame and what's not."

Live theatre has its roots in magic shows, and vice versa. Switching the lights on a scrim (a gauze screen) from the back to the front creates the illusion that something has disappeared. (Take that, David Copperfield.) Shining a light on bits of mirror or aluminum foil looks like fire in a fireplace.

Sometimes magic is simplicity. When I was a reporter on the freebie list in the 1970s, I attended many theatre openings, including out-of-town tryouts for the now-classic *1776, Follies, A Little Night Music,* the James Earl Jones *Othello*, and a grab-bag of lesser shows. Two of the most magical nights I spent in theatre, however, were not those, but were polar opposites in form and content. The first was the 1973 production of Shaw's *Don Juan in Hell* staged by John Houseman with Agnes Moorhead (in her original role of Doña Anna from Charles Laughton's 1952 production), Edward Mulhare, Paul Henreid, and Ricardo Montalban. Houseman had recreated Laughton's elegant but simple staging in which all four performers sat in evening dress at music stands. No props, no lighting effects, just brilliant language and great acting.

The second was the 1980 revival of the Mary Martin *Peter Pan* starring Sandy Duncan as the boy who wouldn't grow up, but who could fly. I spoke to Duncan before the performance and we discussed her particular difficulty. The show featured "flying by Foy," the company that skillfully makes people sail through the air on wires. Duncan, however, was blind in one eye as the result of cancer surgery and so, lacking depth perception, she had to place immense trust in the Foy crew. One remembers that, in rehearsing the original 1954 production, things had gone amiss and Mary Martin sailed full speed into the brick wall of the Winter

Garden Theatre. The next day the stagehands had hung a mattress with the sign "Mary Martin Slapped Here."

"Flying is not easy," Duncan told me with absurd understatement. "They move you up and down, but it's your job to keep yourself facing forward. Your stomach muscles go through a lot." Among her favorite moments in the show is when Peter leads the audience—especially the children—in clapping their hands to keep Tinkerbell alive as the story moves toward its climax. (If I have to explain the plot to you, go back and be a kid again.) Then there was the matter of a special birthday present for crew members on the tour. "That's right," Duncan said, smiling. "When it's someone's birthday, they get to fly. We put you in a rig and send you all over the stage." She grew mock-serious. "After that, they have new respect for those of us who fly."

Boston press night for *Peter Pan* was a mixture of adults, children, and, of course, critics. It's customary for critics to be seated on the aisle so they can make a hasty getaway to file their reviews; even a ten minute delay leaving the theatre can make the difference in meeting deadline. So I was surprised when Elliot Norton, the esteemed critic for *The Boston Herald*, stayed in his seat during curtain calls. Naturally, I did too. And then I saw why. For her curtain call, Sandy Duncan flew out over the audience, right up to the mezzanine, which was full of children. The whole theatre applauded hearing their squeals of joy.

You don't get that kind of magic on YouTube.

Chickens!

IT BEGAN WITH Richard Schickel in 1969. This is when he was film critic for *Life Magazine* and had written a couple of books, one of which, *The Movies: The History of an Art and an Institution* (NY: Basic Books, 1964), had influenced me as a kid making 8mm movies with my friends. It wasn't just his highly readable writing style, it was his ability to place films within their social context and riff about their meaning without becoming stuffy. He became my favorite critic. I was excited, therefore, when it was announced that he would be visiting my university and that I, as a student leader (I ran the highest-profile campus movie theatre), would be invited to his seminar. It was to be a screening of student films and, when the lights came up, Schickel, then 35 and ever the gentleman, spoke a lot without saying anything negative about the clearly amateurish fare.

One definitive thing he did say that stuck with me, however, was an observation I have conveyed to others ever since: "At almost every film festival," he noted (and I'm relying on my memory from fifty years ago), "you see one film after another that's about death, alienation, or politics. They're set in graveyards or empty streets or dance studios. They're depressing and they go on forever. And then along comes a little ten-minute comedy and it wins all the awards because everybody's so happy to be able to laugh." It was the same advice that Preston Sturges embodied in *Sullivan's Travels* (1941) and it still holds true. As Sturges put it, "There's a lot to be said for making people laugh. Did you know that's all some people have? It isn't much, but it's better than nothing in this cockeyed caravan."

Screen Saver Too: *Hollywood Strikes Back*

I kept Schickel's advice in my head for five years after graduation while working as a Boston movie publicist and as a teacher at The Film School at the Orson Welles Cinema Complex in Cambridge. My supervisor was the bright and dryly funny Susan Leeds who somehow lassoed an eclectic herd of filmmakers, critics, and film teachers to work for little money and lots of freedom. Fabled now as "a Mecca for film worshippers" and programmed by the knowledgeable and resourceful Larry Jackson, the Welles Complex at the time attracted a menagerie of young filmmakers, audiophiles, scholars, and other members of the 60s cultural diaspora who had escaped conscription in the Vietnam draft lotteries. Thanks to its passionate benefactors Ralph and Mollie Hoagland, the Welles also had a ton of 16mm production equipment which, as a teacher, I was permitted to use, and a crew of students, which I was encouraged to exploit. Between publicity tours and press releases I wrote a script about poultry taking over the world and called it, not surprisingly, "Chickens!" I structured the script so each scene could be shot in one day without needing any of the actors for a second day. This was important because of who I wanted to appear in it.

"Chickens!" (the exclamation point was important. I didn't know at the time that the term had a second, vulgar meaning) would be cast with Boston's leading critics. As a press agent, I knew them all; as a producer, I figured that, if I put them in my movie, no one would be left to give me a bad review. My crew was extraordinary: Lighting Cameraman Austin de Besche, sound expert Wayne Wadhams, Assistant Cameraman Andrew Harmon, and Editor Bill Gitt. Many of them later shot *The Return of the Secaucus Seven* and *Lianna,* the first films of writer-director John Sayles. In addition, David Keyes handled continuity, Lois Anne Polan did stills, Donald Freed was grip, Steve Sloan was gaffer, and my fellow publicist and close friend Jane Badgers helped as production assistant as well as appearing as an actor. Harvey Appell, for whom I was then working at American International Pictures, let us shoot in his office over a weekend. By luck (mine) and eccentricity (his) producer Jay Ward allowed Super Chicken® to make a guest appearance by sending me an original cel and a signed letter. The only person who turned me down for an appearance was chicken magnate Frank Perdue (who, everybody always said, looked like a chicken).

The cast was a *Who's Who* of Boston's key media figures of the early 1970s. The star was Charles Laquidara, the most influential music DJ on the city's most powerful rock music station, the unstoppable WBCN. Charles played Tommy Yablans, a would-be stand-up comic whose audition for super-agent Lance Steele (Irving J. Hackmeyer) goes so badly that he later returns to sic thousands of angry chickens on him as revenge. "Hack," which is what everybody called him, was the leading time salesman for WHDH, Boston's top AM radio station, and was also a mesmerizing storyteller. Working with him was a scream. He had never acted before and he was a natural. Jess Cain, WHDH's morning drive personality, used to joke that Irving J. Hackmeyer's name was really "Lance Steele" but he changed it to Irving J. Hackmeyer because, "who is going to buy commercials from a salesman named Lance Steele?" You could say that we immortalized him in "Chickens!"

The theme that chickens were taking over the world was a ham-fisted—if you'll excuse the mixed metaphor—way of satirizing racial and ethnic discrimination. To establish the threat of the chicken apocalypse, I staged person-on-the-street interviews with such people as John Koch (Boston *Herald-Traveler*), Madelaine Blais (*Women's Wear Daily*), Arnie Reisman (*Boston After Dark*), Jon Lipsky (playwright), Martin Schechter (commercials), Lois Anne Polan (photographer, later director-producer), Fred Taylor (impresario, Paul's Mall/Jazz Workshop), Treasa Schafer (Welles student), the Bloom family (restaurateurs Fred, Carole, Marty, Laurel), and the Yerkes family (Ira, Jeffrey, Joanne, and Deedee Chereton, publicist), and Mimi and Howard Berkeley (friends). I also made an appearance.

Through the graces of the 57 Restaurant (with whom both Jane Badgers and I had dealt as successive publicity directors of Sack Theatres, the dominant Boston movie house chain), we ad-libbed a fried chicken tasting with "gourmand" Ken Shelton (WBZ-FM, later WBCN) and critic Pat Mitchell (WBZ-TV, later CNN, and later The Paley Center). Finally we picketed the Massachusetts State House demanding equal rights for poultry. Our picketers included Deac Rossell (*Boston After Dark* film critic, later British Film Institute), Mickey Myers (graphic artist), John Semper (*Spider-Man* TV show writer, later creator of DC's *Cyborg Rebirth* comic series), Ken Rogoff (international tour guide and former student director of Boston University's Distinguished Lecture Series), Michael Atwell (Pocket Mime Troupe), and Eric Charlton and Susan Copp (my neighbors).

The jokes were what you'd expect from a social satire. Characters railed against chickens moving into the neighborhood, lamented the fate of capons, made endless jokes about crossing the road, and included a parody of the "News on the March" newsreel in *Citizen Kane* called "Chickens' Lib." What sold it was not the material but the people delivering it.

We held a sneak preview at the Orson Welles Cinema (naturally) where audience reaction confirmed for me that the film worked as intended. Bill Gitt had expertly edited it to a tight 15-minutes, and I started looking for bookings. (I can't remember now why the Welles didn't show it.) Savvy independent exhibitor Justin Freed, proprietor of the Kenmore Square Movie House, agreed to show it as the short subject ahead of a little-known import that Columbia Pictures was releasing in fall 1974. Columbia must not have expected much from their picture because they readily consented to the pairing. The import was Monty Python's *And Now For Something Completely Different* and my picture ran ahead of theirs for an remarkable six months. It's hard to believe, now that Monty Python has become immortal, but "Chickens!" got better reviews than they did. When I interviewed Michael Palin and John Cleese years later for *A Fish Called Wanda*, I strategically withheld that embarrassing (for me) factoid.

The reviews and the engagement were a slight conflict of interest. By the time they ran I was on a special publicity unit for *The Towering Inferno*, and I'm sure that tearsheets reached the Twentieth Century-Fox advertising-publicity department that showed articles about that blockbuster alongside an ad for the Kenmore Movie House featuring "Nat Segaloff's 'Chickens!'"

I'm not saying that, in casting "Chickens!" I had the foresight of George Lucas when he chose his uncannily successful cast for *American Graffiti*. He was brilliant. I just got lucky. But you can judge for yourself; I put "Chickens" on YouTube:

https://www.youtube.com/watch?v=FHIt3AOuu0s

In other words, Richard Schickel was right. My cockeyed caravan was nowhere near as skillful as that of Sturges or the Pythons, but it served its purpose. A couple of years ago I sent a print of "Chickens" to the Academy Film Archive of the Academy of Motion Picture Arts and Sciences where, astonishingly, it now resides alphabetically somewhere to the left of *Citizen Kane*. You can't make stuff like this up.

Screen Saver Too: *Hollywood Strikes Back*

Proxy Producing

CYNICS SAY THAT no good deed goes unpunished. Not to brag, but I have committed several that proved rewarding. While I prefer producing my own documentaries, I have, on occasion, been asked by my fellow producers to help them on theirs, either by interviewing somebody for them out of town or accompanying them when they visit Los Angeles. Filmmakers do this sort of thing for each other and it often proves interesting.

Through Mark Kermode, who I feel is the finest film critic/historian presently in England, I met producers Andrew Abbott and Russell Leven whose company, Nobles Gate, Ltd., was making a documentary on *The French Connection* called *The Poughkeepsie Shuffle*. Both Mark and I were longtime friends with the film's director, William Friedkin. I was interviewed for *The Poughkeepsie Shuffle* and, while I didn't make the final cut (which annoyed me a little given that I wrote the book on Friedkin), Russell and Andrew did ask me afterward if I would go to Baltimore, Maryland to speak with Gene Hackman who won his Oscar for playing "Popeye" Doyle in *The French Connection*. Hackman was in Baltimore shooting *The Replacements* while I was visiting family in nearby Silver Spring, so I drove up to Baltimore to meet the pick-up video crew.

Hackman is a tough interview, or maybe we've just never gotten along. These things happen. While I admire him as an actor, I once made the mistake of telling him so and, as Arthur Penn later explained to me, I broke some kind of rule. Hackman doesn't like being complimented on his acting, so I blew it coming out of the chute. Nevertheless, my one task in interviewing him was something that made no sense to me but was apparently of importance for the documentary. There's a scene in *The French Connection* that takes place on a bitterly cold day as the villain, Charnier (Fernando Rey), enjoys a rich meal in a French restaurant in Manhattan while Hackman and his co-star, Roy Scheider, freeze on the street while tailing him. Hackman blows into his cupped hands to keep them warm. This was the crux of my mission. The hand-blowing. I had no idea why. Perhaps he and Friedkin had a back-and-forth about it when they shot the picture and the documentary producers wanted me to get Hackman's side of the story.

When the opportunity arose during our talk, I duly asked Hackman the question. He didn't understand it. I didn't know how to explain it, so I asked him again, and again he either didn't get it or pretended not to. On my third try he asked me to demonstrate what I meant and I realized that he was playing with me, so I decided to move on, but the fire had gone out and he retreated into years of rehearsed answers. When, a decade later, I asked him for an interview for my Arthur Penn biography, his wife told me that "Gene might answer one or two questions" and that was it. Given that Hackman and Penn had made *Night Moves*, *Target*, and *Bonnie and Clyde* together as well as done live theatre, I politely declined the half-hearted offer and never heard back. (If Gene Hackman is reading this, you are a great actor. So there.)

I never did learn what the hand-blowing business was all about, but it did lead to my being asked to interview Kate Jackson, Cheryl Ladd, and Jaclyn Smith for Nobles Gate's 2000 documentary on the *Charlie's Angels* TV show timed with the release of the theatrical reboot starring Drew Barrymore, Cameron Diaz, and Lucy Liu. Jackson and Smith were two of the original trio; Ladd replaced the third, Farrah Fawcett, who declined to be interviewed. I had never cared about the enormously popular series, which ran from 1976 to 1981. I regarded it as "jiggle" entertainment perpetrated by super-producer Aaron Spelling and my feminist sensibilities were offended. Apparently I had been wrong.

"It was just sheer entertainment," Cheryl Ladd admitted when we spoke, "Three young women who could karate-chop 300-pound guys? We don't know how that could happen. Who would pull guns from who-knows-where sometimes—in this outfit, where did she hide *that*? But all that silliness was what kind of made it fun."[17] As we talked, I started to catch the drift that, whatever the show's producers may have wanted, the show's stars considered their roles subversive.

"We got flack from some of the more stringent Women's Libbers for being a jiggle show," recalled Kate Jackson, "and I thought that they were overlooking the fact that we were three women who were calling the shots on a network television show, in prime time, that was the highest-rated show on, and seen all over the world." Added Ladd, "We got a lot of women, particularly, writing letters to us saying, 'we're so glad that you're doing this show because it's empowering our daughters to feel that they don't just have to be school teachers and nurses and housewives.' Not that there's anything wrong with any of those professions, but the view of women used to be very narrow and what was acceptable for women to be . . . and we changed all that. Women were always portrayed in film as competitive, fighting for the guy, and we were three women fighting for each other."

"I think when they said, 'oh, you're exploited,' it was silly because we really weren't," said Jaclyn Smith. "If you look at what's on the air today it was so mild. You can't over-analyze things. It is what it is. And it worked."

I also had the chance to speak with "Charlie" (John Forsythe) not just about his off-screen presence in the series but about his other work such as two films for Hitchcock (*The Trouble with Harry* and *Topaz*) and a long stage run in a revival of *Mister Roberts*. I wish I had a copy of that part of the tape because his *Angels* material was the least interesting. Forsythe was one of those people who knew everyone and did everything and could shape a story for whatever happened to be the attention span of the medium or the interviewer. They don't make them like him anymore.

Another person they don't make any more are producers like Michael Lennick. Canadian by birth, a special effects artist by passion, and a documentary filmmaker by trade, he usually focused on science-based subjects (*Rocket Science, Dr. Teller's Very Large Bomb*, etc.) but also shot special features for the Criterion Collection, a plum assignment for any film buff, which Michael also was. Thus when he asked me to help him on interviews he had arranged with Gary Zeller, Mark Irwin, and

---

[17] Quotes from Author's interviews for *Three Little Girls*, ©2001 Nobles Gate, Ltd.

Rick Baker (among others) for the Criterion release of David Cronenberg's 1981 *Scanners*, I said "yes" even before he finished the question.

Zeller, an expert in movie pyrotechnics (that means he blows stuff up real good), invented Zel-Jel™ in the 1970s and won an Oscar for his achievement. It's a "protective pyrotechnical barrier gel" (his term) worn by stunt actors and sometimes regular actors who do fire gags. The gel does not burn, so neither does the human wearing it. "I'm a materials scientist steeped in Palmer chemistry and plastics engineering and excelled in creating formulations,"[18] Zeller told us. An expert in explosives as well, Zeller was hired to, among other things, make Louis Del Grande's head blow up for a memorable scene in *Scanners* in which the actor has a "scan-off" duel with star Michael Ironside that sets up the film's theme and horrifies viewers at the same time.

"The problem with pyrotechnics," said Mark Irwin, the film's Director of Photography, "is that squibs can blow something up, but it shows a spark, and . . . you don't want to see that there's an ignition in it." The first try was with a rubber head that they over-inflated with air, "but all that happened," recalled Zeller, "was that we got this ballooning head that just looked ridiculous." They also tried a plaster head and a wax head before taking a life cast of Del Grande, lining it with plaster, and filling it with leftover crew lunches and Karo syrup blood. Eventually they were set to roll but nobody could get the head to explode properly. Finally, Zeller told Cronenberg to start his cameras (there were four to catch the effect) and go hide somewhere while he solved the problem. He crouched on the floor behind the dummy, pulled out a shotgun, aimed it at the dummy's head, and blew the hell out of it with a shell filled with kosher salt. "We settled on kosher salt as the best material for us," Zeller said casually. "Just kosher salt with chunk particles that are crystalline and not too reflective so it couldn't read too well when we blasted at it with this high-pressure shotgun shell. The thing just went all over the place and it looked fabulous. So if ever you want to blow up a head, I advise using kosher salt." Then he added, wryly, "but don't do this at home."

Lennick (with me taking editorial notes) interviewed Zeller in the workshop of the old Mack Sennett Studios at 1215 Bates Avenue in the Silverlake neighborhood of Los Angeles. Built in 1916 (by which time Sennett's discovery, Charles Chaplin, had moved on to the Mutual Film

---

18 *Scanners* special features, ©2015 The Criterion Collection.

Company), its creaky wooden floors and strewn-about props still conjured memories of the very beginnings of the movies. After we left, Michael and I took pictures of each other outside the building, which has been restored and (as we showed) is newly available for production.

Sadly, Gary Zeller died in June of 2014 only weeks after we spoke with him. Equally sad is that Michael Lennick died in November of that same year.

As with other industries, Hollywood is about relationships. The difference is that the relationships you develop in Hollywood are with people that the whole world knows. They say you should never meet your idols because you will invariably be disappointed. They are invariably wrong.

Linda

IT WILL ASTONISH those who think there's a fortune to be made in X-rated movies to learn that the actress who appeared in the most famous porn film of all time got only $1,250, it was taken from her, and it practically destroyed her life. The woman is, of course, Linda Boreman, more widely and tragically known as "Linda Lovelace." The film itself, of course, is 1972's *Deep Throat*.[19]

I met Linda Boreman—who at the time was Linda Marchiano, married to Larry Marchiano—under unusually open and sympathetic circumstances. It was in 1980 when her book, *Ordeal: An Autobiography*, written with Mike McGrady, was published. Her publisher, Citadel, also published *Country Talk* by my Boston radio friend Dick Syatt. Dick and his then-wife, Jane, hosted the Marchianos in their Back Bay apartment and invited me to visit with my tape recorder. At the time, I was Entertainment Editor for the CBS FM station in Boston, WEEI-FM, and Dick's personal endorsement broke a lot of ice with Linda.

I am used to movie actors being smaller in person than one senses from the screen, but Linda (she hated the name Lovelace and said I should use her first name) seemed tinier than her stated five-eight. She was not glamorous in the stereotypical "sex kitten" mold, just wonderfully normal looking, neither sensuous nor tawdry, and had a naturalness

---

19 Readers of *Screen Saver: Private Stories of Public Hollywood* will remember the gauntlet that a Boston movie theatre had to go through in 1974 just to learn that they would be prosecuted if they showed it.

Screen Saver Too: *Hollywood Strikes Back*

that made her truly attractive.[20] The fact that this nice little girl could have been kept, dominated, beaten, and forced by her then-husband Charles (Chuck) Traynor to perform the acts not only in *Deep Throat* but in other even less savory (!) films raised significant issues. Was Linda *actually* trapped, or did Traynor so completely intimidate her that she *thought* she was? How can people, especially men, be made to understand that women in abusive relationships can't "just get up and leave"? At what point do abused women start to think it's their fault and not their abuser's? Add to that the whiff of Mob influence in the porn industry (which Linda said she knew nothing about) and you've got a formula for oppression, even for those female sex workers who insist that they are on the job voluntarily.

Conflictingly, six years earlier in 1974 Linda had published two books (*The Intimate Diary of Linda Lovelace* and *Inside Linda Lovelace*) that spoke well of the porn industry. Presumably coerced or ghost-written, in 1980 they made her a controversial and disputed witness against it. Sitting across from her on the sofa with only a microphone between us, I felt both a connection and a sense of regained innocence. Or maybe I just agreed with her.

Our interview got off to a bizarre start. I had arrived at the Syatts' home from an arduous dental appointment that had required twice the normal amount of Novocain to get the job done. It had not worn off by the time Linda and I sat down together with Jane and Dick watching and Linda's husband Larry stretched out on a couch taking a nap. By this time, the anesthetic had spread to the muscles in half my face and, when I spoke, I sounded like Sylvester the Cat. At first both Linda and I found it funny, but we got serious very quickly as we went over the events in her book, which is to say her life. I used six minutes of the interview for my radio report. What comes next is the first time any of the rest of the interview has appeared:

Nat Segaloff: I'd like to talk about a woman who you used to know. I'm gonna work from that point. And her name was Linda Lovelace.

---

20 I noticed the same thing about Sylvia Kristel, the star of the *Emmanuelle* series, who was a tiny lady with lots of curly hair and nothing to distinguish her in person from any other young woman. On camera, however, she blossomed.

Linda Marchiano: She was another person. That wasn't me. I was a robot at that time doing what I had to do to survive. Now I have the opportunity after nine years to tell my side of the story without getting beaten or have that fear of death over me.

Nat: You were literally kidnapped by a man who was your "husband" and was exploiting you horribly. Did you ever reason to yourself that you'd go crazy if you didn't do something?

Linda: If I hadn't been able to turn off everything that was happening to me and around me, I probably would be in a mental institution today.

Nat: How long were you in that business?

Linda: I wasn't really in the "business" that long. There were a few weeks where there were a couple of 8mms made and then *Deep Throat*. I found it very hard to do.

Nat: The person who brought you into all of this, Chuck Traynor, is now working with Marilyn Chambers.[21] Do you think she's going through the same thing that you had to go through?

Linda: There's a very good possibility. *Philadelphia News* just did an interview with her a little while ago with Chuck—Mr. Traynor—and Marilyn Chambers. They were in a restaurant and during the course of the interview Marilyn Chambers turned to him and said, "May I got to go to the bathroom?" and he said, "No." That's what he did to me, so there is a very good chance that she is going through the very same thing.

Nat: Did they ever drug you or give you anything that would make you unable to think for yourself?

Linda: He just embedded me with so much fear that I just did whatever I was told to do, whatever I was told to say, I said, or I would get another beating. And it came to a point where it was much easier to just do it and get it over with that to keep being beaten.

For a short time, *Deep Throat* became "porno chic" and yearned to cross over from what *Variety* called the "groin grind" adult circuit into mainstream cinemas. It was a fated transition when cities everywhere took it to court and began busting anyone connected with it. Linda found the hypocrisy stunning:

---

21 Chambers appeared in another famous X-rated movie, *Behind the Green Door*, before which she was the model for Ivory Snow laundry soap. The press went wild with the contrast.

Linda: I was in Florida for a court session; I had to identify the movie and they made me watch it. But I didn't watch the movie. I found something more interesting: here I was in an empty courtroom, but when they decided to show the movie the room was suddenly filled with all these busy attorneys and all kinds of people who had other things to do, and judges who left their bench for a few moments. I found it very hypocritical. These are the people who represent justice in our society. A lot of times I was called to different trials for *Deep Throat*. There was one particular time in Arizona when this woman, a lady DA, was prosecuting a guy for running the theatre. He didn't own the theatre, but he did open the door and let everybody in every day. She was trying to put him away for eight years saying how horrible and terrible it was, but the moment I walked in she was like, "Oh my God, I can't believe you're finally here! Oh come on, you've got to sign this for this one." She had me signing autographs and she called people on the phone: "She's here in my office!" She told me that when they confiscated the film they would all come down and show it in the court building and watch it. I found that very disgusting.

Nat: How much money did you make from *Deep Throat*?

Linda: Well, $1,250 was given to Mr. Traynor. I didn't receive anything. See, he felt that if I had money I could make an escape. I was literally held prisoner by him. I wasn't allowed to go to the bathroom by myself, I wasn't allowed to talk to anybody. I wasn't allowed to do anything. If I had money I could escape. The opening scene in *Deep Throat* where I'm driving a vehicle, he's on the floor of the front seat because he felt if I was in the car alone I could make a run for it.

Nat: Do people you worked with try to keep in touch with you?

Linda: No. You've got to realize that it was really like only a three-week period that I was involved in the pornographic world. Which is really sad cuz look what's happened since then. We've gone from *Deep Throat*, which was an accepted film to take your wife to, to child pornography where the youngest victim is seventeen months old to snuff movies where they're actually beating a woman to death. They're committing murder on a film and nobody's doing anything about it. They say they can't figure out who's doing it.

Nat: Are there things that young women such as yourself should look out for if they're approached by somebody? What are some of the ruses?

Linda: I don't think there's any way you could prepare a person for a Chuck Traynor. The most important thing is for parents to keep that door open and to have open communication with their children. Maybe they don't get along some years but there's a time when a child needs a parent and that open door is so important. Let them walk back in it.

Nat: You wrote that you were so eager to get away from your mother that you were willing to do anything to get out of the house.

Linda: That was a mistake I made. I made the decision to go live with Mr. Traynor who, at the time, was coming off like a very nice person. There was no sexual requirement at night when I was living in his house. I had left home, I was 21, I had run a business, I was getting ready to open a chain of boutiques. I was buying a home and a Volvo and I had my act pretty much together, and I wasn't about to move back in with my parents and have my mother say, "All right, you be home by 11 o'clock, call me when you get there and tell me where you are and give me your number in case I want to reach you." I can understand caring, but you can't suppress that much. You have to have trust and make a person feel like an adult. Don't treat 'em like they're fifteen or sixteen again.

Nat: How do you live your life now so you can put everything in the past?

Linda: I'm a happy homemaker. I truly am. I'm into arts and crafts. I'm into my son and my husband and cleaning my house. I have no desire to be an actress. No. Never. I've seen too much of that world to want to have anything to do with it.

Nat: Is there any place for pornography in America today?

Linda: I don't think so. Behind closed doors, maybe. There's a great deal of difficulty when you get into censorship and completely taking people's rights away. But there should be a limitation. Remove it from the view of the eye. People that patronize X-rated theatres or bookstores, they know what's inside. There's no reason to put it on the outside where children can see it. And not just children, but men and women who find it offensive. I recently had a girlfriend who took her brother into a store, the brother is fourteen years old, and there's one of our more accepted sexploitation magazines. On it was a woman bound and it said "Women flirt with pain." And this guy turned to his sister and said, "Do women really like pain?" Now, I'm not a psychiatrist or a psychologist, but that's damage. He probably would have grown up, married a woman, been very happy, and not even thought about that. Now it's in his head: "Oh maybe I should go beat up a woman; they like it." That's what they're doing, and it's not right.

Nat: Why does pornography mostly involve women?

Linda: I think the people who do it hate women. Maybe when they start putting men bound and chained on the cover of a magazine something will be done about it. Men will stand up and say, "Hey, wait a minute." When I hear, "It's the First Amendment," my God, I get angry. The First Amendment was not written to protect pornographers. I'm sure they didn't have that in mind. And for them to use that—they don't care about that. It's the farthest thing from their mind. All they're caring about is the dollar.

Nat: *Ordeal* is written by you and Mike McGrady. What sort of questions would he ask?

Linda: When I would leave something out, he would have to ask questions. He was just as embarrassed asking them as I was to go through it.

Nat: It's a very difficult book to read, not only because of what you're going through, but because your dialogue is very explicit in many cases. Is not this, in a way, pornography?

Linda: The most important thing there was to let people know exactly what I was going through during my time of captivity— the language I was hearing, the attitude of the people around me at that time. That was very important. You'd be surprised how many people don't know what's in an X-rated movie. There are people who don't know that people are naked, let alone the explicitness of them. That's very important. As a human being you must make yourself aware of it. If people read *Ordeal* they can eliminate themselves from having to see an X-rated movie. But you have to have the knowledge. If half the world had knowledge of what goes on, they would put a stop to it. The people who don't know are letting the pornographers overrule them.

Linda's story haunts me, particularly in light of the anti-women comments made during the 2016 Presidential campaign and the contortions performed by various partisans, including religious leaders, trying to justify them. Pornography vs. violence against women and the First Amendment vs. censorship are ongoing struggles, but when you see them played out in the eyes of someone who has been dragged through the minefield it takes on a name and face. I seldom request autographs from actors, but I always do for authors and, when my interview with Linda was over, I asked if she would sign my copy of *Ordeal*. She wrote, "To Nat—Linda." When she handed it to me, I said, "How come only your first name?" and she replied. "Linda Lovelace is dead."

It might be said that if Linda hadn't had bad luck, then she wouldn't have had any luck at all. Whatever kind it was, hers ran out on September 22, 2002 when she died following a car accident. She had sued Chuck Traynor for divorce in 1974, married Larry Marchiano that same year, and divorced him in 1996, also claiming abuse. In her life she had been mistreated by her parents, used by both the porno industry and the anti-porn lobby, and been turned into a thing. The $1,250 she was paid for making *Deep Throat* had been confiscated by Traynor. Her life after that was half-scandal, half joke, and zero concern for who she really was. She was fifty-three when she died; I had met her when she was thirty. That was several lifetimes ago.

Screen Saver Too: *Hollywood Strikes Back*

On the Shoulders of Giants

ARTISTS, SCIENTISTS, and others speak of standing on the shoulders of giants in recognition of those whose earlier efforts informed theirs. In my case, I sit at their feet. When I wrote that I placed myself at Arthur Penn's feet so I could look up at him while I was writing his biography, I mean it literally; during one interview session he took the sofa and I found it more comfortable sprawled on the floor. (Yes, he offered me the chair.) I remember thinking at the time, "I won't have to lie when I tell this."

That wasn't the only instance when I sat quietly while a filmmaker I respected held forth, though most of often it was at eye level. Meeting so many of them, first as publicist, and then as journalist, and later socially, I always made it a point to ask one or two questions for myself that I never intended for public consumption. Call it an *ad hoc* film school. Here are some of the lessons. (Where there are direct quotes it's because I saved transcripts; where not, I saved memory):

- Arthur Penn (director): When you're auditioning actors for the stage, always call them back, even if they give a good audition. Unlike film, stage actors have to give eight performances a week, so you need to know that their audition wasn't a quirk and that they can repeat it.

- John Chambers (special make-up artist): If an actor gets a pimple you can't cover it with makeup, but you can work with the Director of Photography and the lighting people so that you don't cross-light it. You use flat lighting that minimizes it. (Today, of course, they can digitally remove blemishes.)

- Dom DeLuise (actor): People's energy flags in the afternoon so you want to have some kind of meat or protein for them to munch on.

- William Friedkin (director): You want to know when to cut from shot to the next? You hold on a shot as long as it's good, and then you cut to the next one.

- Mark Rydell (director): Mark and I were watching *The Black Stallion* (1979) on an airliner. It's the story of a boy and a horse who are shipwrecked on a tropical island and then, when they're rescued, he becomes its jockey. Rydell, who had directed a cast of kids in *The Cowboys*, watched it intently and realized of the boy, "He can't act." He then began a shot-by-shot analysis describing how director Carroll Ballard and editor Robert Dalva didn't hold on the boy, Kelly Reno, for a complete sentence. They would start on him and then cut to another actor, or start on another actor and then cut to him. Sometimes they would carry dialogue between the other actors and play it on the boy's placid face. "It's called constructing a performance," Rydell said, adding that this is sometimes necessary when an actor is physically correct but is an unskilled performer.

- Roddy McDowall (actor): McDowall starred for John Ford in *How Green Was My Valley* (1941), a sentimental tale of how time and progress doom a Welsh mining community. McDowall had several emotional scenes and was constantly frustrated that director Ford always said "cut" before he could complete them. Time and again he would rehearse the scene right up to the point of release, and then they would stop. When they finally did shoot the climax, all the performers let out their pent-up emotions on the first take, which is exactly what Ford wanted. Said McDowall in praise of Pappy, "He played us like a harp."

- Woody Allen (writer-director-actor): A comedian makes a bargain with the audience in the first few minutes of a film so that, if a laugh comes every thirty seconds, he has to keep up that pace for the rest of the film. Also: the first draft of a joke will probably be the one that works because it springs pure from your brain. You can play with it as much as you want, but most of the time you'll go back to the first version.

- Ralph Bakshi (animator): Notoriously fractious, in truth Bakshi is just passionate. His films had a realism in their performances that other animated films seldom matched. I asked him whether animators grow tired of drawing the same character hundreds of thousands of times over the course of a two-year production schedule. On the contrary, Bakshi said, they wish they could start over again because by the end they really understand the character. "Animators are very special people," he said, and added that he was blessed with good animators. "You have to understand what an animator's head is all about: sitting there and making it come to life. That's their dream, that's their love." As for the performances he achieves, he told me to stand up and tell him I didn't want to sit down. Then he told me to sit down. I wouldn't. He said it louder, so I responded louder, "No." "Why not?" "Because we're doing an interview." We overlapped. He smiled. The he said, "See? I've just directed you. That's how we do it."

- Will Vinton (Claymation® innovator): Working in the malleable medium of clay, Vinton and his crew (some twenty-two people when their studio was a-hoppin') found that clay has a subtlety that is not present in models or cels, which is what other animation studios use. "There is something really astonishing about clay when it's moving," Vinton said. "Gradual changes in expression work like flesh—it's flowing, changing, shifting—unlike cel animation." Like a lot of young filmmakers, I started off animating clay dinosaurs and I found that they tended to melt under hot lights. Vinton said he had the same problem and that they had to sculpt a new character for each shot, not just each scene, and that the eyes and mouth are critical for making expressions. Of course, all of this has been changed by the advent of digital imaging, but there's still something wonderfully hands-on (symbolically as well as literally) watching Vinton's early work like "Closed Monday," "The Little Prince," and "Vanz Kant Danz."

- Saul Zaentz (producer): Speaking of "Vanz Kant Danz"—the John Fogerty song written in protest of accounting practices that Fogerty said Saul Zaentz's Fantasy Records used with Fogerty's musical group Credence Clearwater Revival—producer Zaentz, for me, was unexpectedly accessible. With Oscars for *One Flew Over the Cuckoo's Nest* and *Amadeus*, you'd think he would have holed up in his San Francisco offices, but no. He was always approachable (even though he passed on my script). When I was doing movie publicity (*Cuckoo's Nest*) he was the first person to ever give me a thank you gift: a belt buckle with a flying bird. I still have it. I also have Zaentz's admonition that mediocrity never guarantees success. "You have to take risks," he said pointedly. "Sure you can fail, but sometimes you will soar."

- Robert Radnitz (producer): Radnitz also took risks by making films with good taste. He signed for me a poster from *Sounder*, "Find your own way." He didn't mean "do it on your own," he meant that everyone who succeeds in the film business—*really* succeeds—has done it by discovering a path that no one else has trod. For him it was making films that appealed to children without condescending to adults. Such successes as *Sounder, Where the Lilies Bloom, Cross Creek* and a personal favorite, *A Dog of Flanders*, attest to Radnitz's eminence. When we worked publicity for *Where the Lilies Bloom*, he got off the plane wearing his trademark tennis whites (sans racket). When I saw him for the last time it was at the opening of a play in Los Angeles directed by our mutual friend Leonard Nimoy. I hardly recognized him, not because he had aged (haven't we all) but because he was in normal clothes. I spent time telling him how much he, his films, and his advice had meant to me. Later word got back to me that he had been moved by what I'd told him. His last film had been the TV movie starring Leonard as Mel Mermelstein, the man whose lawsuit against a Holocaust denier

Screen Saver Too: *Hollywood Strikes Back*

established the legal proof of the Final Solution. The movie was called *Never Forget*, which is painfully ironic because so many people have forgotten Robert Radnitz.

- Stirling Silliphant (writer): although I handled Stirling and his wife, Tiana, on press tour for *The Towering Inferno* (which he scripted), our friendship truly took hold years later when I was profiling him for *Backstory 3*, which I later expanded into his biography, *The Fingers of God*. Stirling was a compulsive (and well paid) writer but one tidbit stood out from all the advice he gave me and it's something I taught my screenwriting students for years: Just sit down and write the goddamn script. Or, as he put it more delicately, "A script should take no longer to write than it will take to shoot." Once you've worked out the structure and characters, if you write three to five pages a day, and most films take eight to twelve weeks to shoot, you're on track.

- Richard Chew (editor): The man who co-edited *Star Wars* (with George and Marcia Lucas and Paul Hirsch) knows something about putting pieces of film together, but I wanted to know whether there was a difference between editing comedy and editing drama—other than leaving some, but not too much, space for the laughs. "Comedy is even more complex," Chew said, "because, in addition to telling the story, you have a whole other layer of jokes. The jokes can help or hurt your timing of the scene. It's a minefield. You want to keep the jokes but not lose sight of the story." My other major question—again, this was one for me and not for the public—was whether he had to change his style between a standard-frame film and wide screen. The answer was yes. "The larger screen presents so much more information that it absorbs a lot of the time so that you do have to give more allowance for it. The larger the screen, the more time it takes for the audience to find what's relevant."

- Albert Whitlock (matte artist): The publicity folks at Universal couldn't understand why I wanted to interview Albert Whitlock for my newspaper. They knew who he was, but felt the reading public wouldn't. I didn't care; I wanted to talk to the man who showed us what Los Angeles looked like after being leveled in *Earthquake* (1974) and had created dozens of other invisible effects. A matte is a big painting on glass that's mounted in front of the camera. It can add a skyline, create a landscape where none exists, and extend the height of sets that are only built to one story. In the decades before CGI, mattes added blazing skies and impossible building perspectives. "With mattes, sometimes less detail is more," the gentlemanly Whitlock said. "You want to give the *impression*. And of course you don't stay on the shot too long." Whitlock made his painting of LA in ruins look more realistic by scraping small spots of paint off the glass and setting up smudge pots at various distances on Universal's back lot. Seeing the smoking smudge pots through the holes in the matte gave it a convincing depth.

- Volker Schlöndorff (director): When I saw his early film, *Young Torless* (1966), which describes how peer pressure and passivity can create conditions that lead to fascism, I was stunned by his handling of such a volatile subject. I finally had the chance to meet him after he had directed *The Tin Drum* (1979), another parable for Nazism. I admired him and his films, so I don't know why I had the gall to ask, "What was it like being German and walking into a costume shop with hundreds of Nazi uniforms hanging there?" His answer surprised me. "There weren't any," he said, explaining that they had to make all of them from scratch for the film. He reminded me that relics of the Hitler era were destroyed or banned, including movie props. (I didn't have a second helping of gall to ask what they did with the costumes afterward.)

- James Bridges (writer-director): "Color is important," he said. We were discussing his 1978 film, *September 30, 1955*, in which Richard Thomas bravely plays a young man so obsessed with James Dean that, when Dean is killed on that date, he leads his friends in a rebellion without a cause. The studio (Universal) wanted to tone down the character to keep Thomas, who was also playing John-Boy on TV's *The Waltons*, more likable, but both Thomas and Bridges held fast. The color red, Bridges said, signifies danger in the film. A red car, red props, and red clothes (Thomas wears a red

Eisenhower jacket like Dean at the end) all have meaning. "When I was planning this with the costume department at the studio," Bridges recalled, "they told me that the only other director who wanted such control over the use of color was Alfred Hitchcock." Bridges had begun his screenwriting career by writing for the *Alfred Hitchcock Presents* television series. Talk about standing on the shoulders of giants.

Becoming

"WHAT MAKES *you* a film critic?" I used to get asked this question more often that I heard, "Paper or plastic?" Depending how it's asked, it's not a question, it's a challenge. Here's the answer: I became a film critic because someone hired me to be one.

That someone was Clark Smidt. I was walking through Harvard Square in October of 1977 when Clark pulled over in his large (for someone who grew up in the 60s) car and asked me what I was doing these days. He knew damn well I was on *Evening Magazine*, and it was Clark's sarcastic sense of humor that made us friends. He asked me if I wanted to be the film critic on his radio station. I said, "Why not?" I thought he was still Program Director of WBZ-FM, the Westinghouse music station in Boston, where I had brought many a celebrity for his main announcer, Ken Shelton, to interview when I was a Boston movie publicist. I had met Clark through Ken, and I had met Ken when he was a grad student at Boston University's School of Public Communication while I was an undergraduate there. Turned out that Clark had left WBZ-FM, to become Program Director at WEEI-FM, the CBS-owned music station, with studios on the 44th floor of the Prudential Tower ("The Pru") rising like a square spike jammed into Back Bay Boston. I visited him there, we easily agreed on terms, and he called my segment "Tuning in on the Movies." In time I would come to write, record, and produce twenty separate features each week: ten reviews, five brief interviews, assorted weird stories from the syndicated "Odyssey File," and one heavily produced lifestyle feature called "Under the Boston Skyline." I was given complete control of content, respecting only the FCC and CBS's standards of decency, which were reasonable. It was heaven. I worked there from November 1977 to January 1981 and turned out some 2,000 pieces. It was there that Ken Shelton gave me the nickname I have used ever since: *Nataloff.*

All of the above is by way of explaining what made me a film critic. Good contacts and dumb luck.

Okay, I did have credentials. I'd studied film, but so had half of my generation. My advantage was that by the time Clark hired me, I had worked for distributors, exhibitors, and private agencies. I knew something about the business of film as well as its aesthetics. I had also—and this is where my peers and I had the advantage over our colleagues today—watched the most exciting generation of filmmakers since World War Two develop artistically. We grew up with the French New Wave. We watched Italian cinema shift from Neo-Realism to its "white telephone" incarnation. We marveled at the emergence of new German, Dutch, and Czech cinema. We rediscovered previously ignored American auteurs and celebrated upcoming ones. It was the age of the director, a ten-year period when people went to the movies to see what was new and what was old, not what was remade, rebooted, sequeled, or franchised. We watched De Palma, Herzog, Scorsese, Schrader, Altman, Mazursky, Penn, Truffaut, Rohmer, and Fassbinder grow up. We watched Bergman, Peckinpah, Fellini, and Kubrick mature. Each new movie was a discovery, not a rehash.

Most established critics in the 1960s had held their jobs for decades and viewed motion pictures more as literature than as film. This is understandable because most of what they reviewed was heavy on dialogue and music with rare exceptions like Welles, Hitchcock, Curtiz, or Mamoulian, who knew from the start how to move the camera and had a sense of "cinema." Only with the advent of the film school generation did critics bring to their jobs a knowledge of the changing grammar of the screen, and it wasn't all verbal. I was one of them. My colleague Gerald Peary has made a documentary about this period and more called *For the Love of Movies* that I think does a better job than the Roger Ebert movie, *Life Itself*. In those days, Roger wasn't *the* critic, he was *a* critic. He was local (Chicago), and he was one of many working critics who loved their jobs because they loved movies. There were dozens like him, and they were very good, but he and Gene Siskel were the lucky ones who got the national TV show.

This was the world I entered when I started broadcasting on WEEI-FM. Clark had designed the Softrock format (which others adapted without offering him either credit or royalties) that was heavy on Linda Ronstadt, James Taylor, Fleetwood Mac, Billy Joel, and Judy Collins, and deaf to Sex Pistols, Ramones, and early metal groups. At the same time, we avoided show tunes, folk, and old standards unless they were covered by a new artist. I once asked Clark why we never played Leonard Cohen, who was a personal favorite of mine, and he said, "Because we don't want our listeners committing suicide." Our target demographic was men and women 18-49, the prime spending group, and we achieved our goal more often than not. The trick, though, was not just attracting them but holding them through multiple commercial breaks. People tend to listen to radio for the music but switch channels when commercials interrupt the flow. Clark's skill was integrating the spoken features within the music and commercial tapestry to create a programming flow, and the happy result was that—according to Arbitron, one of the two ratings services we used—listeners stayed put on our signal for an average of an hour and fifteen minutes. This was remarkable. Or maybe it meant that more hip dentists listened to WEEI-FM.

Part of this success came from the station's unusual marketing. Our symbol was, not surprisingly, a rainbow (well before rainbows and unicorns became hackneyed). Our advertising slogans stressed easy listening over hard rock, i.e., "Joni (Mitchell)—without the Baloney," "The Beach Boys—Without the New Wave," "The Eagles—Without the Turkeys," "The Moody Blues Without the Blahs" and one that never flew for me, "Linda Ronstadt—Without Wondering What Blew By You" (her hits included a cover of Roy Orbison's and Joe Melson's 1963 hit "Blue Bayou." Get it?). That last one was nearly responsible for a CBS meltdown. In early 1980, Clark and Ray Welch, the brilliant Boston-based advertising man, designed a contest whereby listeners would be invited to add their own "this . . . without that" entries to the thirty that Softrock was already using. 117,000 letters came in, swamping our mailroom, and we intended to sort through them ourselves to pick a winner that was both witty and consistent with our playlist. The prize was a suit from Louis, the high-end Boston haberdasher. When the CBS brass in New

Screen Saver Too: *Hollywood Strikes Back*

York heard these naive plans, they panicked that the contest might run afoul of FCC contest rules. They demanded that we find an objective independent firm to do the judging. We did, someplace in Rhode Island, and those poor souls winnowed the 117,000 entries down to a final 75 from which Welch chose the Moody Blues while our station people went with Ronstadt. CBS was mollified.

We were also Boston's first automated station. Since this was before mp3 digital files, we put the songs, commercials, and features on hundreds of audio cartridges (like 8-tracks except they worked) and stuck them into a massive wall of playback slots in a system called BIG HERM. BIG HERM was our computer. She took up a huge air conditioned central cell sealed behind sliding glass doors in our studios. When new music came in and was approved for airing by Jim Spellmeyer, our Music Director (in concert with Clark), one of our engineers—Bob Cook, Larry Vidoli, or Lou Guilford—would dub it to cart, encode it with subsonic beginning and end frequencies, and load it into HERM. Our announcers never touched vinyl records, although we did have turntables for off-air production work. Instead, announcers pressed a button to trigger the cart playback. DJs had no input into what they played. Instead, Jim and Clark handed each of them (I say "them" because I was in the news division and only did air shifts in emergencies) a printed list of songs in the order in which they were programmed. It sounds confining, and perhaps it was, but the format worked.[22]

The air staff included Ken Shelton (natch), Hillary Stevens, Jay Gates (Quentin Migliori), Mark Bashore, Bill Smith, Debbie Ruggiero, Don Cohen, and Dick Gunton. I was told that Dick, who was older than the rest of us, was hired as part of a union settlement when the station went to automation, but I can tell you that we were the lucky ones. His professionalism was unflappable, especially in light of my brief tenure as his sassy news reader.[23] Jim and Clark sometimes went on the air, too, as

---

22 Most of the time, that is. When it came to overnights and weekends, the DJ prerecorded all his or her segments ahead of time and went home. If HERM ever got out of sync, it was programmed to play the Beatles' "Help" as a signal for the engineer-on-duty to rush over and fix it. "Help" was only to be played as an SOS.

23 In an attempt to boost ratings it was decreed that I should deliver news with "attitude," a spectacular misjudgment. How spectacular? Well, in an anniversary story about the 1970 Kent State massacre I referred to the National Guardsmen who had killed four students as murderers; caught the giggles when reading a story about police

did News and Public Affairs Director David Austin, whose interviews not only met the station's public service commitment but our unwritten social and moral responsibilities. Another on-air contributor was Paul Erickson of the New England Aquarium who offered environmental features.

Considering how corporate CBS was, our low-pressure work environment was remarkable. Although we didn't do chummy company picnics or Boston Harbor cruises, every couple of months our genial but straight-laced General Manager Jack Baker would sport for dinner in a private room at the Harvard Club where, lubricated by good wine, we declared our everlasting love for one another. It wasn't *WKRP in Cincinnati*, but we had fun. Lou Guilford was forever asking us to sample "Mrs. G's Tartar Sauce" that he was trying to market. Debbie Ruggiero would show up with big pots of homemade fettuccini Alfredo. I was known to fire up a hotplate and make quart after quart of steamed clams. Maura Mulcare, who started as receptionist-production coordinator, had an inexhaustible supply of Cheez-It crackers that she readily shared. (Maura later married Clark Smidt and had two children, Jeffrey and Katie.)

Like any broadcaster seeking free labor in exchange for school credit, we had interns. Some, like Steve Bosselman and Pierce O'Neil, I brought in from Boston College, where I was teaching. David Austin acquired others, one of whom, Michael Bright, became Program Director of competing rock station WFNX and later moved to other markets.

We were a tight young group. When Jack Baker deemed things to be in order on many Friday afternoons, he took to leaving the station early and we broke out the wine and called it a Jack-Off Day. For a rock music station in the late 70s we were remarkably free of drugs (and if you think I'd ever say anything different in print, you're probably doing them).

We stayed on the air during the blackout of New England's devastating Blizzard of '78 because the ever-prepared CBS had a generator that kept our signal going. This meant that I could still record my 20 weekly program inserts regardless of the fact that the Pru's elevators were out. This meant that, after trudging miles through the snow from home to the Pru, I had to climb the forty-four flights of stairs to our

---

breaking up a cockfight; and wrapped a report about a factory manager trying to stop employees from using company bathrooms as "the number one and number two story in the news." I was younger then, okay?

studio, practically in the dark. When I'd finished, instead of going down those forty-four flights, I climbed an additional six to the fiftieth floor where WBCN-FM was off the air (they didn't have CBS's foresight). That didn't mean that the DJ wasn't on the job. With no music, no lights, and no heat, we kept warm by lighting a fire. At the end of a joint. When I got home some time later and listened to my recordings on the air, I discovered that, operating on reduced power, the Ampex tape machine I'd used had run at a slightly slower speed. The result, when the pieces were played back at proper speed, made me sound like I'd been doing lines instead of reading them. When the elevators worked again the next day I returned to re-record everything.

As always within a corporate structure, there were downsides. As a member of the respected CBS News division, I was forbidden to do commercials. I watched as one announcer after another went into the booth to record advertisements and make extra money. Not me. Indeed, when it came to CBS policy (and we're talking about a time when Edward R. Murrow and Walter Cronkite were spoken of with reverence), news people couldn't make product endorsements (with the exception of my reviews where the practice was understood). We couldn't accept freebies without declaring them to management. Finally—and this still applies to people who work in the broadcast industry—we were not allowed to take part in audience or ratings surveys. I still use this to cop out of telephone surveys.

Language was also important. A program was never "brought to you by" an advertiser, it was specifically "sponsored by." On Fridays we had to say "partly sunny" instead of "partly cloudy" when giving weather reports because "partly sunny" sounded more upbeat for the benefit of our advertisers.

CBS began falling apart in 1985 when Atlanta broadcasting mogul Ted Turner pulled a greenmail attack on the company, messing with its stock price, and Lawrence Tisch stepped in to save it. Unfortunately, the cost of buying back the stock that Turner had inflated drove the network into a downward spiral. The news department, which in those days was not a profit center, suffered.

But by then I was long gone. David Austin had replaced Jack Baker as General Manager and a new Program Director named Rick Peters had replaced Clark Smidt. One Monday in January 1981, Rick called me into his office to ask me why I had reviewed a German film called *Taxi Zum Klo* (*Taxi to the Toilet*), an X-rated, gay-themed independent movie that I wasn't particularly enthusiastic about, but which had opened at a major Boston theatre and therefore had to be covered. Peters let me know that the station was no longer interested in reviewing "that kind of film" and I was now to submit all my reviews to him before recording them. Naturally that was unacceptable, as he knew it would be, and we came to an immediate parting of the ways. As I left, David Austin promised me four years' worth of severance pay, then had to call me later to say that Rick had stopped the payment because I was only a freelancer and not entitled to it. He was right of course, but it hurt David, of whom I was fond, to have to break a promise to a friend. David was a good man.

Some time after that, David died of cancer. Jim Spellmeyer and one of our salesman, Jerry Lester, had preceded him, also with cancer. Lou Guilford had to have a lung removed. Cancer again. Many of us kept getting colds and bronchitis. We had worked on the 44th floor of the Prudential Tower with its sealed ventilation system, atop which were fixed most of the microwave antennas for Greater Boston. Four cancers in a staff of fifteen or twenty people is an extraordinary coincidence. We asked our landlord to investigate. They said there was nothing to it, nothing at all. Our landlord was the Prudential Insurance Company that owned the building.

The years pass. At this writing, WEEI-FM is an all-sports station. The ratings are huge. The only way I can explain this is by trying my own slogan: "All Sports—Without the Jocks."

Screen Saver Too: *Hollywood Strikes Back*

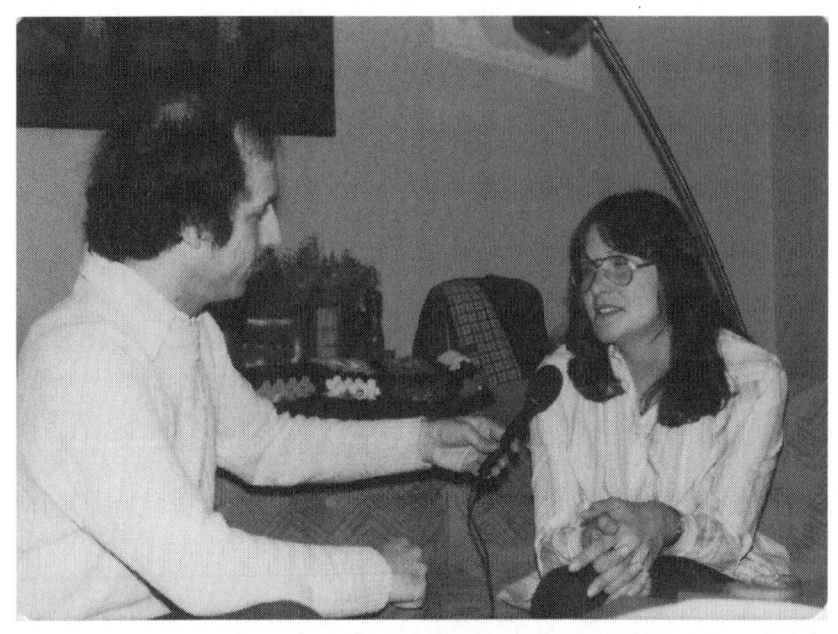

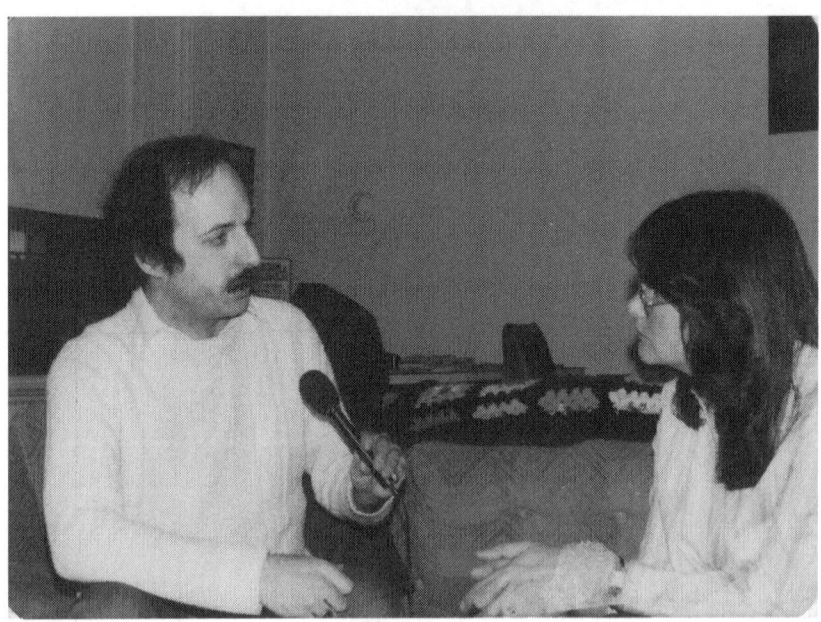

The Author interviews Linda Marchiano, February 20, 1980 (photos by Jane Syatt)

Photographs 79

Michael Lennick at Mack Sennett Studios March 14, 2014 (photo by the Author)

The Author (as Charlie Chaplin) at Mack Sennett Studios March 14, 2014 (photo by Michael Lennick)

Marty Sender and Robin Young co-hosted WBZ-TV's Evening Magazine in Boston. (Video frame enlargement, 1977)

Screen Saver Too: *Hollywood Strikes Back*

(L-R) The Author, director William Friedkin, Evening Magazine co-host Robin Young, and star Peter Falk on the set of The Brink's Job *(1978) (photo by Josh Weiner)*

The Author interviews a wary Charlton Heston for The Mountain Men *(1980).*

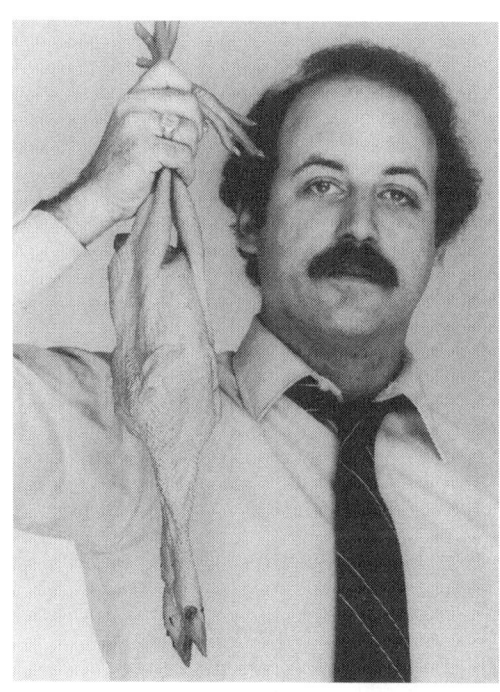

The Author in a publicity shot for "Chickens!" (Author is on right) (photo by William Smith)

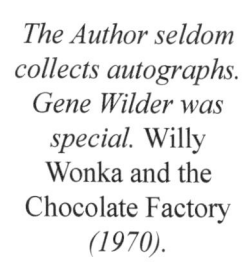

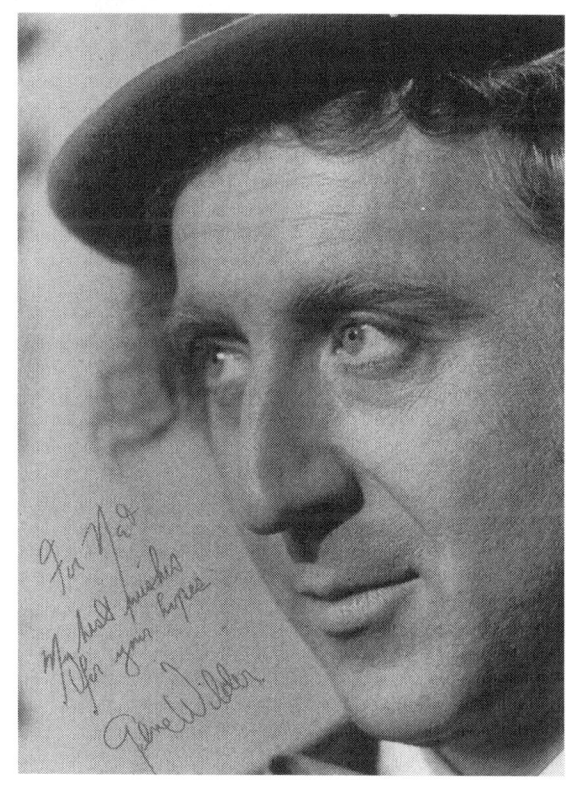

The Author seldom collects autographs. Gene Wilder was special. Willy Wonka and the Chocolate Factory *(1970).*

Screen Saver Too: *Hollywood Strikes Back*

Peter Cushing wanted to die but fate made him live.

Dustin Hoffman and presenter Ben Stiller at the 2004 Bill of Rights award dinner of the ACLU of Southern California (courtesy ACLU-SoCal).

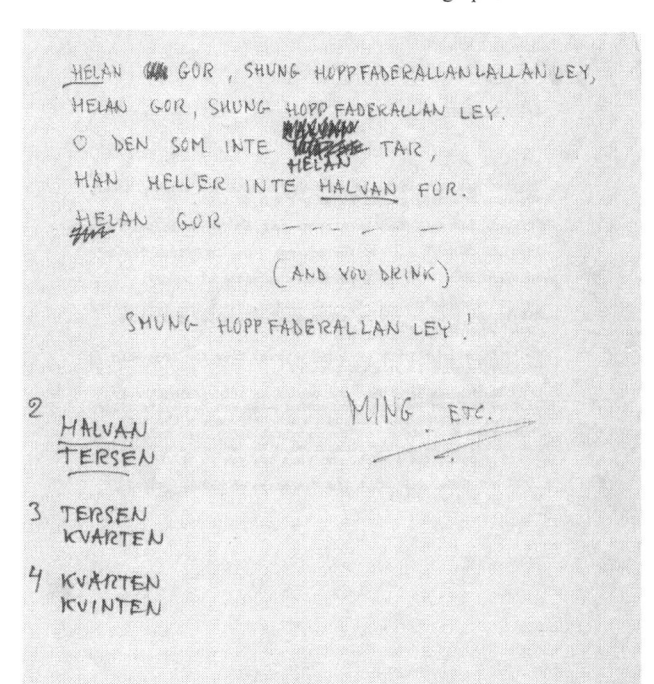

HELAN GOR, SHUNG HOPPFADERALLAN LALLAN LEY,
HELAN GOR, SHUNG HOPP FADERALLAN LEY.
O DEN SOM INTE ~~HALVAN~~ TAR,
              HELAN
HAN HELLER INTE HALVAN FÅR.
HELAN GÅR
~~///~~
              (AND YOU DRINK)
SHUNG HOPP FADERALLAN LEY!

2 HALVAN   MING ETC.
  TERSEN

3 TERSEN
  KVARTEN

4 KVARTEN
  KVINTEN

Max von Sydow's handwritten lyrics for "Helan Gor" (1980)

Sonny Grosso (left) and Eddie Egan (right) appeared in The French Connection, *the film of them making the biggest heroin bust in history. Sonny later became a producer, which is how the Author met him.*

Screen Saver Too: *Hollywood Strikes Back*

Evening Magazine *"Tipsters" were encouraged to be creative. For* The First Nudie Musical *the Author reviewed the movie in a barrel in Harvard Square (1977). For* The Greatest, *he fought his way out of a paper bag in midtown Boston. Hey, it got me into TV, didn't it?*

Butterfly McQueen was a surprise dinner guest and an even more surprising interview subject. (Photo Wiki Commons.)

Director Mark Rydell, one of the best film teachers the Author could ever want even if we hadn't been trapped on an airplane watching a movie with the headphones off.

Screen Saver Too: *Hollywood Strikes Back*

Robert Radnitz, the eccentric producer who made some of the best-ever non-Disney family films including Sounder *and* Cross Creek.

John Landis, probably the best comedy director since Blake Edwards.

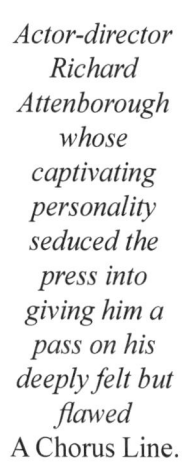

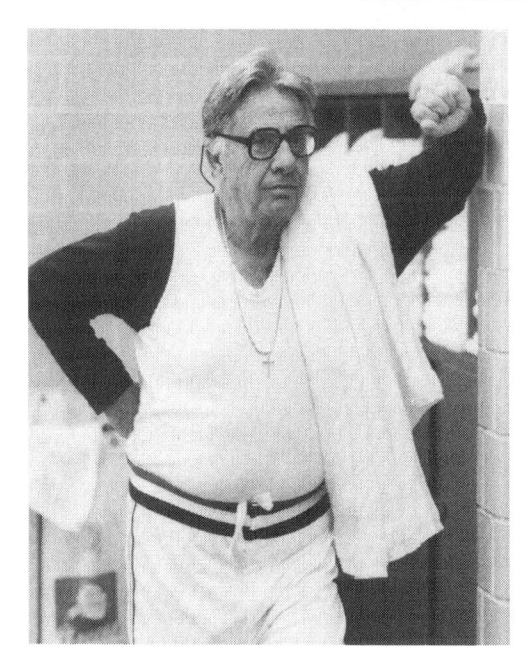

Actor-director Richard Attenborough whose captivating personality seduced the press into giving him a pass on his deeply felt but flawed A Chorus Line.

Socially conscious filmmaker Martin Ritt, who was also a friend.

Screen Saver Too: *Hollywood Strikes Back*

Everything in this picture that isn't a musician, an extra, or Barbra Streisand is the massive New York Street from Hello Dolly *that stood for years inside the entrance to the Twentieth Century-Fox lot on Pico Boulevard in West Los Angeles.*

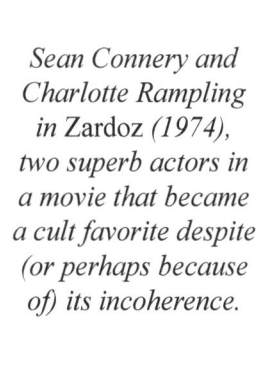

Sean Connery and Charlotte Rampling in Zardoz *(1974), two superb actors in a movie that became a cult favorite despite (or perhaps because of) its incoherence.*

Martin Ritt and Robert Radnitz attend a fundraising event for the ACLU of Southern California (ACLU photo by Sydney Lee)

Talk Was Cheap

IF YOU'VE BEEN comparing my timeline in this book with those in *Screen Saver*, you will have noticed that some of the stories overlap. This is not a mistake. As a freelancer, I held several jobs at once; as a freelancer, you *have* to. From 1976 to 1991 I wrote hundreds of pieces for *The Boston Herald*. From April 1977 to November 1979 I was a tipster and producer for some 100 video features for *Evening Magazine*. From November 1977 to January 1981 I was Entertainment Director for WEEI-FM, a job that yielded some 2,000 reviews, interviews, and features. Somewhere in that span I also wrote several episodes for the WCVB-TV comedy series *The Baxters* and a movie special called *New England's Great Entertainers*. From 1982 to 1985 I was a reporter and producer for WSBK-TV's *Movie Loft & Company*, the interstitial program that followed that super-station's nightly feature film (except when the Red Sox were playing). From fall 1978 to spring 1980 I taught at Boston College, and from spring 1980 to fall 1990 I was an instructor at Boston University. Oh, and from somewhere in 1978 to 1980 I was an overnight talk show host on WITS-AM. There were probably a couple of magazine articles squeezed in there, too.

If it sounds like a lot of work, it was; if it sounds like a lot of money, it wasn't. Local rags and broadcasters don't pay freelancers much. Even AFTRA, the broadcast union, had minimal concern for freelancers since the big dues were earned by the Big Names such as news anchors and staff announcers. This changed somewhat as cagey companies switched their staffers to contractor status in an effort to minimize union influence. Freelancers never had fringe benefits or job security. And while, in theory, a freelancer can turn down work, in reality you hoard as much of it as you can for when it slows down, as it inevitably does. Many's the time I wished I had held a nice, comfortable staff position at any of the places for whom I freelanced. But it was never in the cards.

I also had the arrogance of youth. I figured I could always get work. In a tightly knit town like Boston, one thing always leads to another once word gets around that you know what you're doing. But it was still a struggle whenever a new editor replaced an old one or a broadcast station changed formats. There was a fine writer named Gerry Nadell who dominated Boston's freelance market in the 1960s and 70s. His primary byline was *Women's Wear Daily*, but he also wrote for *Boston Magazine*, the *Boston Globe*, and everywhere else. He was a brand name and he was also a friend. Tragically, he had a heart attack in his early 40s and died. And this is how freelance works: before he was even in the ground, every freelancer in town knew that the market had opened up and started pitching Gerry's editors.

When I got a call from Chief Engineer Billy McCarthy at WITS-AM, I had to look up where the station was, same as I had with Clark Smidt. I also wondered why a Chief Engineer would be calling me about an on-air job. I quickly learned that, at WITS, the lines of authority were a squiggle. WITS was formerly WMEX where I had brought many a celebrity in my press agent days to be interviewed by their colorful host Andy Moes. Joe Scallon, a sports-obsessed businessman, had bought the broadcast license and the single-occupant, two-story building in Boston's Bay Village and turned it into a source for "Information, Talk, and Sports—W-I-T-S." With 50,000 watts at 1510 on the AM dial it boasted a good, clear signal. But that was only during the day. At night they had to cut it to 5,000 watts so as not to interfere with other stations broadcasting in other states at 1510. After sunset, the ionosphere takes on different reflective properties, so AM stations bouncing their signals off of it tended to leach into each other. Needless to say, 5,000 watts doesn't travel as far as 50,000 watts. In fact, it's just a notch above hooking up your antenna to a radiator in your dormitory to pull in your college carrier wave station.

If the weather's good—that is, if the ionosphere is on your side—your signal might make it from Boston to Quincy.[24]

Now that I think of it, WITS was strange. Strange but lovable, like the wacky neighbors on a sitcom. Its physical location was at the nexus of three of Boston's least compatible neighborhoods. In one direction was Skid Row where homeless and inebriates dwelled; it was not uncommon to find men passed out in our doorway on cold mornings. In another direction were several gay bars which, in those Gay Lib days, were not only out of the closet, they were partying in the street. Then there was Film Row where the film companies had their regional sales offices. It would be safe to say that WITS was in, but not of, the neighborhood.

Not being a sports person, it was clear that I was going to be handling talk and entertainment. They even threw in restaurants. My visibility on *Evening Magazine* didn't hurt either (once again proving the axiom that the best way to get a job is to already have a job). My prime slot, which we called "Behind the Scenes," was a show business call-in and interview show that aired Saturday night from 8 to 10 PM between Harley Gordon's legal advice show and Bill Grundfest's comedy show.[25] The second was a Thursday overnight call-in show about restaurants. The restaurant show came about because I had been writing the "Cheap Eats" column for the *Boston Herald*. This was called synergy. I called it exhaustion.

There's a sidebar to this that needs telling, if only to show how newspapers work. The *Herald*'s long-time food critic was Gus Saunders, a capable writer and a stylish man (he wore cravats), who was also a radio broadcaster with whom I had booked many celebrity interviews as a press agent. When the *Herald* editor offered me the food column in the paper's new weekend preview section, the first thing I asked was, "What about Gus Saunders?" I was told, "Don't worry about Gus Saunders." Feeling uneasy, I left the office and whom should I meet in the lobby but Gus Saunders. I said, "Gus, have you got a minute?" and pulled him aside. I related what had just happened upstairs and right there we made a

---

24 It also made for some nasty phone calls when the station, which carried the Red Sox games, had to cut its power in the third inning, pissing off tens of thousands of passionate sports fans.

25 Bill would soon move to New York and open the highly influential Comedy Cellar on MacDougall Street in Greenwich Village. An extremely talented writer and stand-up comedian, he later became producer/writer for the Paul Reiser-Helen Hunt TV series *Mad About You* and other hits.

pact that I would write about the business of restaurants more than about the food, and we would never overlap. In this way the editor couldn't play one of us off against the other. Gus continued his high-end reviews and I happily spent the $25 expenses the *Herald* gave me every week on Chinatown dives, neighborhood bars, and sandwich shops. It also kept me from looking like the inexperienced freelance dilettante that I was. I did it for two years and 25 pounds, then gave it up and went on a diet.

With that backstory, I rolled into WITS to learn the audio control board and their call-in system (I was to be my own engineer as well as producer). I already had my Third Class FCC license and I was good to go.

There is no feeling in the world like being the only person in an isolated radio station in the middle of the night. At least Wolfman Jack in *American Graffiti* had Richard Dreyfuss and a fridge full of melting Popsicles to keep him company. Moreover, our weak signal meant that the pool of listeners who could hear the show, and the even smaller pool who were inspired to call in, was below tiny. Capping it was the fact that WITS was a sports station and didn't attract the crowd that experimented with restaurants. What we did attract—and you can bet your ratings I kept them on the line as long as I could—were restaurant owners, wives of restaurant owners, brothers-in-law of restaurant owners, and people who had friends who were restaurant owners. The ratings were so low that we didn't even draw the usual call-in kooks. And now that I think about it, I hardly had any commercials to read so the sales department must have been hip.[26]

The other "I" (information) programs on WITS earned their keep. Dick and Jane Syatt hosted an immensely popular dating show called "Hotline" where they connected people, talked about dating, and held meet-and-greet events. Dr. Joy Browne, a psychologist, was just then beginning her long career in on-air relationship counseling. Lanny Daley, a warm and delightful Boston Brahmin (Lansdale Chatfield) with a show business bent and absolutely no pretentions, hosted a talk show and reported on city events.

---

26 Let me say for the record that, between the *Herald* and WITS, I came to regard running a restaurant as the toughest profession there is and I have enormous respect for those who do it well.

Our most unusual air personality was Bob Hudson. Nicknamed "The Emperor," Bob had been half of the popular KGBS Los Angeles morning team Hudson & Landry in the 1960s. Bob Hudson and Ron Landry's on-air banter and scripted skits were compiled on a series of best-selling comedy albums and a string of TV guest appearances. In 1967 a quiet but intense USC film student named George Lucas shadowed Hudson for several weeks to make a short film called "The Emperor" which showed him at a number of locations, not just KGBS, and preserves a record of his bravura personality. The Hudson-Landry partnership ended in 1974 when they split up to work at a succession of radio stations across the country, including WBZ-AM and WMEX in Boston, but never again together. By the time I met The Emperor at WITS (nee WMEX), he was a shopworn middle-aged man. Of course, I had heard of Hudson & Landry—as a kid in Washington, DC, I grew up on their comedy records—and it was painful to reconcile their lively spontaneity with the tired Emperor who lived in Studio A and left immediately after his sign-off. The years, the drink, and the gambling had taken their toll. He enlivened his afternoon show with tape playbacks, fake phone calls, wisecracks, and characters, all of which he produced during the workday for use during his shift, but he was a man out of his time. Almost as soon as I arrived he was replaced by a sports talk show. He tried several straight announcing gigs elsewhere after that but, my god, he was Emperor Hudson, not some generic announcer. He died in 1997 at 66. But in truth, he had died twenty years before.

Hudson's leaving made it possible for WITS to commit to sports, a smart move in Boston, one of America's top sports towns with the Celtics (basketball), New England Patriots (football), Bruins (hockey), and Red Sox (baseball). WITS carried the Bruins and Red Sox games and came under massive criticism for firing Red Sox announcers Ned Martin and Jim Woods after the 1978 season. Glenn Ordway, the magnetic announcer for the Celtics, also appeared on a WITS call-in show.

But the piece that completed Joe Scallon's puzzle was "Clif 'n' Claf." "Clif" was Clif Keane, the Boston *Globe's* acerbic sports columnist. His on-air partner "Claf" was Larry Claflin, Keane's *Boston Herald* counterpart. Clif and Claf were formidable and competitive, and callers were as apt to be shot down as encouraged. They swung wide and wild, frequently skewering players and management alike. They were also a handful at the station, so much so that they were often called, behind their backs, "Syph and Clap."

Keep in mind that these were the days before computers, Google, and data banks. Producers, air personalities, and callers had to keep sports statistics in their heads or know how to rifle through a Bill James book to find what they needed. They did remarkably well and, when they didn't, that made for good air talk too.

Despite the male slant at the station, my closest friends there were women. I ran into Phyllis Guarnaccia quite literally: she was barreling out of an office as I was entering the hallway and we collided. A fiery Sicilian from suburban Boston, raised in a family dominated by a father and brothers, she was out to prove herself as a director. Because we both knew and loved film, we hung around together and continued our friendship when each of us moved to Los Angeles in the late 1980s, becoming a two-person support group in that inhospitable city. Since then, Phyllis has worked on numerous television shows and at least one short subject, "Fait Accompli," about a strained relationship shown in flashback, which she and I co-wrote.

My other woman friend at the station was Jennie Paul who had the toughest job of all: she was a female sports reporter in the male-dominated field, and she was doing it at a radio station where testosterone practically shot out of the drinking fountains. Jennie is the only daughter of Gabriel Paul who was President and part owner of the New York Yankees the year they brought the World Championship back to New York. Needless to say, she had a depth of sports knowledge to rival any of the men on the air and an inexhaustible list of contacts to call upon. As an example of the latter, I once walked quietly into Studio B where she was interviewing someone on the phone. I was there to fetch a record for a radio drama I was producing when she signaled me to join her. "Do you know how to sing 'Back in the Saddle Again'?" she asked, knowing I was a fountain of entertainment information. "Sure," I said, and she held up the phone receiver so I could croon into it. It's a good thing I trusted her (I still do) because after I'd finished the first verse she went back to her call without saying anything and I left the room. Later she said, "Do you know who I was talking to?" I didn't. "That was Gene Autry." At the time, Gene Autry was the owner of the Los Angeles (later Anaheim) Angels baseball team. Before that, in the 1930s, he had been the movie's most popular singing cowboy, had made scores of films and serials (including *The Phantom Empire*), and was my favorite western star when I was a kid. "Back in the Saddle Again" was his theme song and I have the embarrassing distinction of having sung it back to him on command.

Jennie's brother, Henry Paul, also worked at WITS, which was a good thing, because she was under ridiculous pressure and needed him. Jennie is an author whose remarkable book *The Yankee Princess* tells of growing up in in a home where she had to compete with the New York Yankees for her father's affection. At this writing, she and I are trying to turn her book into a movie that we describe as "a female *Field of Dreams*."

One of the WITS adventures was a series of original radio dramas I wrote, produced, and directed (which means I stood there and said "we're recording") for my Saturday night time slot. Taking a cue from NBC's *Saturday Night Live*, which was new and funny at the time, we called our drama troupe The Not-Ready-For-50,000-Watt Players. I wrangled my friends and anyone else who had an ego and a voice to appear in these things which included a satire on the awful Dino De Laurentiis remake of *The Hurricane* that we called *The Drizzle,* and an ambitious but depressing story about a faded journalist on a fading journal titled *Newspaper Picture*.

They loved it when I covered current films. When *Animal House* came out, I threw an on-air toga party (read about it in a later chapter). On another night I placed a call to filmmaker James Bridges who was scouting locations for *Urban Cowboy*, getting a scoop on Gilley's bar and its mechanical bull a year before all of them hit big. We aired an oral history of the Orson Welles Cinema on its tenth anniversary that survives as the only record of that historic enterprise. The purpose of these gambits, plus occasional documentaries and many taped interviews, was to fill the two hours on a Saturday night when nobody who had a social life would want to come to the studio for a live show. The irony that escaped everyone except the sales department was that anybody sitting at home on a Saturday night listening to radio was not an attractive demographic because he or she was, well, sitting at home on a Saturday night.

I'm not sure whether I left WITS or WITS left me. It was that casual, and my affection remains. I do know that, in 1983, the station began a dispiriting succession of name and format changes, ultimately (in 2014) resuming its old call letters WMEX. I have to say that there was joy in being paid to do radio when you know nobody can hear you but you still hope they can. Arthur Godfrey said that the secret of good broadcasting is to remember that people listen as individuals, not as groups. I once suggested that, rather than broadcast, we should just phone both of our listeners and do the shows for them. Nobody could hear me say that because I said it after sunset. But boy it was fun radio.

No Comment

WHEN I WAS A PUBLICIST I used to advise my clients, most of whom were film personalities, that the best way to avoid answering an interviewer's embarrassing question was to simply say, "I'd rather not answer that, thank you" and then shut up. This works better on live TV and radio where the host's fear of dead air is greater than the celebrity's fear of answering. Print interviews are less time-based but no less subject to silence. The point is that even seeing "Mr. X refused to answer" is a lot safer than what might have made it into print if he had. Very few interviewers will come right out and ask, "Do you still beat your wife?" But they will fly remarkably close by asking, "How many of those divorce rumors should I believe?" Even denying it poses a risk because it will then have been addressed. Better to say nothing.

Ernie Anderson, who was Louis Armstrong's personal publicist and promoter before he joined John Huston's retinue, told me that Satchmo had a trick for getting the press on his side without going on the public record. He would invite them to his dressing room for drinks and tell such filthy stories that nobody could print anything, so they just wrote about what a terrific guy he was. It also works for politicians. Mike Weiss, the movie press agent and one of my mentors (see *Screen Saver*), spoke of a similar trick when he said, "all Presidents become great movie fans," and explained how a Chief Executive will invite fifty people to a screening in the White House theatre. He'll greet them all as they arrive, watch the movie with them, and then say goodnight on the way out. Meanwhile everyone can say that he spent two hours with the President and the President hasn't had to exert himself making small talk.

When I became an interviewer, I had to outwit my own cautionary advice. Sometimes this involved saying, "Lovely weather we're having" as a way to break the ice I had just formed with a question my subject didn't want to answer. I don't do ambush interviews but sometimes I accidentally step in someone's poo. Most of the time if I really wanted an answer, I would return to the question in a different form a little later in the interview. As a last resort, when the interview was over, I would apologize and, more often than not, the celebrity would answer the question, thinking that we were off the record. In point of fact, the interview isn't over until the reporter leaves the room.

Now that I've written how to avoid giving answers, let me give ten tips on how to get them:

1. Research. Just as no trial lawyer should ask a question to which he doesn't already know the answer, so should an interviewer prepare by studying what the subject has previously answered (or not answered). "Did you really say that the only way to end the world's problems is with an absolute monarchy?" I asked John Milius, who was known to make provocative statements. "I've changed since then," he admitted, "Unless I'm the monarch." He was clearly joking about both, so I didn't use either.

2. Break the code. You may know all about the celebrity but the celebrity knows squat about you. Chat a little. Talk about who you both know in the business. Compliment his or her film, play, book, music, etc. (if appropriate). You have to establish your credibility. I once got actor Robert Carradine's attention by telling him that he reminded me of Peter Dekom. Dekom was one of Hollywood's most skilled lawyers of whom few people outside the industry would normally be aware. "Hey, wait, I know him," Carradine said, and started taking me seriously.

3. Hold off asking important questions as long as you can. The first twenty to thirty minutes of an interview are pretty much useless because the celebrity will be giving you the same stock answers he's given everyone else. It takes most of them about half an hour to run out, and after that is when you get the good stuff. This presumes that you have a long enough time slot; indeed, many interviews are kept short precisely so they never get into anything below the surface. Gene Wilder and I had

run out of things to say after we'd spoken about *Willy Wonka and the Chocolate Factory*. It was early in his career and I felt a warmth in him that put me enough at ease to ask a completely inappropriate question: "Do you like your movie?" Surprisingly, Gene gave me an unexpected answer: "They made it 60 percent for children and 40 percent for adults and I thought it should have been the other way around—40 percent for children and 60 percent for adults. The book (*Charlie and the Chocolate Factory* by Roald Dahl) is very nasty, you know, but the film wasn't." I remembered this conversation when I saw Tim Burton's remake with Johnny Depp. Depp missed the point in his portrayal but the rest of the film was what Dahl intended.

4. Off the record versus on the record: be scrupulous, but set conditions. I always tell my interview subjects, before I start my tape recorder or roll video, "If you want to take something off the record, please tell me right away so I don't have to go hunting for it." Sometimes, after the interview, you can go back and ask them, "You know, that stuff you took off the record wasn't that bad, would you like to put it on the record?" Often they say yes. When I interviewed William Peter Blatty, a meticulous and scholarly writer as well as one of the warmest men I have ever met, he took certain answers off the record. Afterward, I sent him the transcripts—I often do this for fact-checking, particularly for books—but I purposely didn't mark what was on and what was off. (I kept an annotated copy just to be safe.) Seeing it objectively and on consideration, he made minor changes for clarity and kept almost the whole thing on the record. (Bill, wherever you are, if you're reading this now, thank you.)

5. Translate talk into type. When people see a direct transcript of their speech, they freak. Lauren Bacall once took me to task for making her sound illiterate ("I wrote a *book*, for God's sake!") and I had to remind her that the transcript I just handed her to go over was not the finished article, it's the way she spoke. She immediately hunkered down and made corrections. I've only known a handful of people I could quote without editing: Paul Newman, John Milius, Erwin Chemerinsky (Founding Dean of the UC Irvine Law School), Alan Friedberg (former VP of Loew's Theatres), Joseph L. Mankiewicz, and a very few others. Most people talk themselves into verbal cul-de-sacs and have to be res-

cued in editing. You can always tell during an interview when the subject wanders off track and tries to get back on again. If you're doing the interview for print, you can usually fix it. Video is tougher. Garry Marshall was a warm and achingly funny man, but I don't think he ever reached the end of a sentence. He was tricky to edit for sound. When I hear a quote spinning out of control, I usually say, "Would you like to say that again" or, if you're feeling generous, "I didn't understand that; could you put it another way?" The subject always appreciates it and, quite often, you'll get something better. Producing that documentary on Darryl F. Zanuck that I declined to discuss earlier, I had to stew while the director interviewed Roddy McDowall, one of Hollywood's best storytellers, but who had the flu and could barely sit up, let alone concentrate on what he was saying. Knowing that his labored responses would make him look bad on the show, I occasionally interrupted and asked him to repeat his answer. The director blew up at me but it saved the interview.

6. Appear protective. I hate this trick, but sometimes you have to use it. When doing video interviews with stars on press junkets, they usually allot you ten minutes: two to set up, seven for the questions, and one to get out the door. Many a star gets slap happy at the meat parade; answering the same dumb questions is like doing the same take fifty times. What I have been known to do when sitting down, but before they say "we're rolling," is to tell the star, "pull your jacket down in back" or "do you want to fix your hair?" This tells the celebrity that you're looking out for his or her best interests.

7. If at first you don't succeed, ask, ask again. It never hurts to re-ask a question that wasn't answered the first time. And then ask it again if it still isn't answered. Just do it after you have all the other material that you need in case your subject bolts. On an NPR interview with David Hyde-Pierce of *Frazier* the reporter asked an off-the-wall question that made them both laugh. Said the journalist, "I was going to make that my last question," to which Hyde-Pierce replied, "And so you have."

8. The old "is there anything you'd like to say that I haven't asked?" trick. If you ask this toward the end of the celebrity's long day you're very likely to get something that neither of you had planned on and is

perhaps better than what came before. That's where the Charles Grodin quote came from at the front of this book. We had been discussing the film he had just written and starred in, *Movers and Shakers* (1985).

9. Talk to someone else. Actors crave attention. No matter what they say, they cannot abide being ignored. Wait and they shall come unto you. For the movie *Halloween*, I was booked to interview producer Debra Hill but my editor really wanted me to speak to the film's star, Jamie Lee Curtis, who had come to town with her. Jamie Lee's publicist, however, said she would be too busy and too tired to talk with me. When I arrived in their suite to interview Hill, Jamie Lee was packing. As I engaged Hill, out of the corner of my eye I could see Jamie Lee working her way closer and closer to the sofa where Debra and I were having a lively conversation about John Carpenter. I continued to ignore her until, finally, she sat down between us and insinuated herself into the conversation. I got my story. I have worked with her several times since then and she is still the naughty, quicksilver smart woman she was when she first became a star. Sadly, Debra Hill died in 2005.

10. The nuclear option. If the celebrity staunchly refuses to answer your questions and you honestly believe that you were fair and asked politely, the only thing you can do is bluster, "Why did you agree to an interview if you don't want to say anything?" If they won't answer that either, get up and leave. It's over. This happened to me only once. The celebrity was not only unresponsive but sullen as if I'd committed some terrible crime by just showing up. After ten minutes I finally said, "Thank you, I don't think we have anything to talk about" turned off my tape recorder, and left the room. His publicist, whom I knew well, was waiting in the hall and asked, "What happened?" I said, "When you find out, please tell me." I never took him on in print, nor shall I name him here because he is still alive. And he's probably still an asshole.

It's important for the interviewer to maintain control of the conversation, but sometimes the subject has an agenda that he or she will not relinquish. Usually this happens with politicians who know that if they give you an answer, any answer, you'll have to use it even if it's not the answer to your question. Celebrities are different, but sometimes they throw you.

In an interview with Billy Dee Williams for *The Empire Strikes Back*, we were halfway through our half-hour schedule when he blurted out, "Hey, what's going on with the public school funding in this town?" Newspaper stories had revealed yet again that less money was being spent on schools attended largely by children of color. I was momentarily thrown by Williams' hijacking of the interview, but by then we both knew that we had talked enough about *Empire* and that the picture didn't need more publicity, but that school funding did. It also didn't hurt to have Lando Calrissian as an advocate for education.

John Brady, when he was editor of *Writer's Digest*, wrote a book called *The Craft of Interviewing* (NY: Vintage Books, 1971) which goes into helpful detail about landing an interview as well as conducting it. More recently, Lawrence Grobel wrote *The Art of the Interview: Lessons from a Master of the Craft* (NY: Three Rivers Press, 2004). Their advice seems overly polite in today's Twitterized world where celebrities are stalked and their privacy is invaded as if it's the public's right to know everything about them. No wonder they have clammed up or instructed their publicists to demand signed agreements from interviewers setting the terms and conditions for access. (I've never signed one of those.) In the movie *Manhattan*, Woody Allen and Marshall Brickman wrote that gossip is the new pornography. It seemed an overreaction at the time (1979) but has since become true (including about Allen). While I never want to return to the heyday of the old-time fan magazines whose fabricated articles were lies invented by studio flacks to create screen images for their contract players, I would like to know a little more about the movies and a little less about the Kardashians, the Biebers, the Jenners, and the Hiltons. The problem with media whores is not getting them to talk, it's getting them to shut up. It was Paul Newman who put it into perspective for me in 1981 in those innocent years before the social media explosion. I was co-interviewing him with a colleague who pressed the superstar a little too hard. I forget the question, but Newman's answer was, "Whoa, this is just a movie okay? We're not curing cancer."

De-Clawing the Critics

TIMES HAVE CHANGED since Harold Ross, founder and editor-in-chief of *The New Yorker*, told film critic Nunnally Johnson that "reviewing movies is for old ladies and fairies." There are very few old ladies reviewing films these days. In fact, there are very few of anybody reviewing films any more, not in the serious sense. Newspapers, radio, and TV stations are cutting their film critics (along with other entertainment coverage) on the misguided belief that reviews are just free advertising, that the public no longer heeds critics, and that websites do the job. Simply calling out the editors and program directors who make such short-sighted decisions is not harsh enough. They are quite simply destroying the soul of society.

Artists struggle to create works that speak to the human condition. Their enemy is the crass mechanism that decides what art gets made and whether it ever reaches its intended audience. The performing arts (theatre, dance, music, and film) are massively expensive enterprises and require the support of paying audiences, benefactors, or the government. But benefactors are mercurial and government grants come with worrisome strings, so these arts must appeal to the public. Paying audiences, however, are choosy with their time and chary with their money. Whom can they trust to guide them? Critics, of course.

In the beginning of the twentieth century when the movies were young, they were a novelty, and novelty was enough to draw newspaper coverage and curious patrons. Within a few years, however, the novelty had worn off and the theatres showing movies had to buy ads to attract audiences. The emergence of the star system helped; pictures with stars made more money. Then along came film critics. Some sources credit Frank E. Wood as America's first film critic. Wood wrote briefly for *The New York Dramatic Mirror* before being asked by D. W. Griffith, whose groundbreaking films he had favorably covered, to help him adapt Thomas W. Dixon's racist novel *The Clansmen* into the equally racist masterpiece, *The Birth of a Nation* (1915). Whether Griffith hired Wood for his talent or to neutralize him as a critic is open to debate.[27] By the emergence of the modern studio system a decade later, film critics were an entrenched lot, although they were more like consumer reporters in that they generally just described films without judging them. This was because motion picture advertising had become a large part of a newspaper's revenue stream. At one point some newspaper's advertising director must have sat down with that paper's entertainment editor and realized that the free space being given to movies in publicity was greater than the space that the theatres were paying for. This is when formulas were introduced. The Hearst papers were frank about entertainment accounts getting half as much free space as they bought in paid space. Movie ad rates were also increased to make up for the "loss," even though coverage of movie stars sold papers.

The studios by the late teens and into the twenties had perfected their ability to build stars and manage their popularity. In addition to making pictures, stars were profiled in newspapers, and PR stories about them were planted in the growing number of movie fan magazines such as *Photoplay* (founded 1911), *Motion Picture Magazine* (started in 1914), *Picture-Play* (founded 1915), and *Screenland* (begun in 1920). These gave the ticket-buying public the supposed inside scoop on the darlings of dreamland and probably lured more than one poor sucker to California in search of stardom. They were also closely managed by the studios. The effect of these public relations tools was to counteract the growing

---

27 Hollywood has a history of hiring its critics to write films, the most effective of whom include Nunnally Johnson, Frank Nugent, James Agee, Jay Cocks, Paul D. Zimmerman, Paul Schrader, Roger Ebert, Paul Attanasio, Richard Schickel, Stephen Schiff and the entire French New Wave. Peter Bogdanovich may be the most famous modern critic-turned-filmmaker, but he liked to claim that he was always a director who was merely working as a critic. Pauline Kael was famously hired by Warren Beatty in the mid-1970s to advise him, then got shunted to Paramount but quit when they wouldn't listen to her and went back—sadder but no wiser—to reviewing.

problem of people who were watching movies and then telling the public whether they were worth seeing. These were film critics. Until Graham Greene in the late 1930s and James Agee in the 1940s, very few critics dared actually write anything as negative as most average people said when they discussed movies in person. It was considered unseemly. Even a negative notice was free publicity and, besides, it disappeared the next day while the movie ads continued and got bigger on Sunday.

Film companies endured critics for seventy-five years. On one day they would complain that their big-budget film was being reviewed unfairly, and on the next day they ran quote ads for a sleeper that they would have shelved if not for the critics' attention.[28] Although Gene Siskel and Roger Ebert deserve much credit for pointing out ignored films, scores of less visible critics across the country had been doing the same thing for years, only not on national TV.

Starting about 2010, things flipped. People stopped reading newspapers and began getting their reviews from places *like Rotten Tomatoes, Dark Horizons, Ain't It Cool News*, and dozens of other websites and blogs. The joke was that a kid could tweet a bad review of a new movie before the last reel had made it onto the screen, and the film would die before the projectionist could pack it back up in the shipping case. Suddenly the only credentials anyone needed to review a movie was the fact that he had bought a ticket. Since their young audiences lacked sophistication, blogs and bloggers were made for each other.

The other factor that sounded death knells for critics went by the name "synergy." This took place when the corporations that had been buying up the old line movie studios in the middle 1960s diversified even further by buying newspapers, magazines, publishing houses, radio stations, record labels, cable TV companies, and television networks. Not only did this result in the radical reduction of competitive sources of news and information, it set in motion a situation in which one end of a media conglomerate created the product while another end employed people who criticized it. How foolish. The answer, of course, was to get

---

28 I was present at Twentieth Century-Fox the morning after Peter Bogdanovich's Cole Porter musical, *At Long Last Love* (1974), starring Burt Reynolds, Cybill Shepherd, and Madeline Kahn, opened soft. That afternoon Fox's advertising vice president said, "Let's get out the Burt Reynolds campaign" and ordered Bogdanovich's sophisticated ad concept scrapped in favor of one that made the paper-thin love story look like an action romance.

rid of critics. At first Hollywood rejoiced. They had finally made critics superfluous. With so much money being poured into blockbusters that were engineered to meet the lowest common audience denominator, the last thing the film companies wanted was anyone who knew anything about movies to call them on it. What nobody predicted was that, with theatres becoming only one of several platforms to see movies, audiences were getting picky. Going to the movies had become expensive. Two people spending $100 for tickets, parking, and concessions is not uncommon today versus $20 for the same thing only a generation ago. So the film had better be good. Only now there's nothing but the rumor mill to find out.

Professional film critics may have been hard to deal with, tough to please, occasionally wrong, and aesthetically demanding. But they knew what they were doing, they had clear standards, and they were in the profession for the long haul, not just to draw a social media following. There now exists no dependable support system for Hollywood product—or, for that matter, independent cinema, which needs it more—other than multi-million dollar advertising campaigns. Somebody should have told the film companies to accept the advice they so often used in their own pictures: be careful what you wish for.

Images

IN HIS BOOK of the same title,[29] Peter Bogdanovich quotes James Stewart as saying, ". . . That's the great thing about the movies . . . After you *learn*—and if you're good and Gawd helps ya and you're lucky to have a personality that comes across—then what you're doing is—you're giving people little . . . little, tiny pieces of time . . .that they never forget." Audiences aren't the only people who are privileged to see the pieces of time that Stewart names (and of which Bogdanovich himself has created so many). Those of us who work in the picture business, even at a low level, come away with mental snapshots—private moments—that transcend their context. Usually they are magic, but sometimes they can be discomfiting or just downright weird.

I can't understand how famous people can feel comfortable revealing personal information to total strangers, but they do. I entered the hotel suite of director/stunt coordinator Hal Needham expecting to do an interview for his new film *The Villain* (1989) and found him sitting sidesaddle, his legs flopped over one arm of a hard desk chair and his back pressed against the other. "Are you okay?" I asked. "Yeah," Needham said, "it's just the damn hemorrhoids." Where do you go from there? I'll tell you. Writer-director James Toback and I were sharing a bottle of Sancerre and talking about his theory of film when he began discussing his prostate problems. It was a lovely Sancerre, dry but not biting. A year later I was interviewing actress Lucy Saroyan (William's daughter,

---

29 *Pieces of Time*, NY: Ann Arbor House/Esquire Books, 1973.

Walter Matthau's stepdaughter) and Toback's name came up. "How well do you know Jimmy?" she asked. "Well, we discussed his prostate over wine," I said. "Well," Lucy smiled, "then I guess you know Jimmy."

When I was a publicist, they sent me Charlotte Rampling with precious little time to arrange interviews. Her film was *Zardoz*, and she happened to be in New York doing national publicity when my Fox contact, Nico Jacobellis, called to say that he was lending her to me for a day in Boston. She arrived two mornings later with her husband, Bryan Southcombe, and their child, Barnaby. Southcombe, she said as she presented him to me, was the man who had introduced the Beatles to Maharishi Mahesh Yogi. As stunning as Rampling has remained over the years since that encounter, in 1974 she was all of 27 and heart-stoppingly beautiful. She handled her interview duties with the professionalism I have always respected from British actors, even attempting to explain what *Zardoz* was about. The image I shall always retain of her, however, is the one I saw as I arrived at her Ritz-Carton hotel suite. Bryan ushered me in and said, "She's getting ready now," just as she emerged from the bedroom wearing a *Blazing Saddles* T-shirt with incredibly tiny iridescent blue panties barely peeking out from underneath it.

When I first met Arnold Schwarzenegger he wasn't yet a movie star, although that was certainly on his dance card. He had just co-written *Arnold's Body-Shaping for Women* and his Simon & Schuster publicist, Saul Gilman, had asked me to do an interview. As a multi-honored Mr. Universe, Schwarzenegger was treated as a curiosity by the press—until they met him. Once you got past his obsession with body building, he was an immensely funny, charming, and perceptive man. Knowing this about him is what jump-started my conversations with writer-director John Milius about *Conan the Barbarian* (1982). The stereotype of body builders is that they are muscle bound ("the beach is that way," etc.), but Arnold dispelled me of that image with his earnest conversation and one physical move. We were in his hotel room and his phone rang. Standing next to it, he swept his right arm in a grand arc as if making a move in a competition and lifted the receiver up to his ear, all while continuing to look me in the eyes. Think of it: he knew at all times where the phone was and where his hand was going, like a cat stepping over the stuff on your desk without having to glance back. And he never lost concentration. Some people are just stars.

Former (1950) World Middleweight Champion Jake LaMotta and his estranged wife, Vicki, got back together to promote *Raging Bull* (1979). The Champ—why call him Jake when there aren't many people you can call Champ—described how Peter Savage's biography *Raging Bull* filled in the backstory of why he had been so self-destructive in the ring and in his life, something missing from the movie. Despite the picture's renown as the best film of the 1970s, many people feel that this lack of motivation prevents understanding Robert De Niro's portrayal of LaMotta. The reason: when he was a punk kid, La Motta thought he killed a man. Years later, the man showed up sitting ringside, and LaMotta, out of guilt, relief, and penance, allowed himself to be pummeled into hamburger by his opponent. This closed the emotional door of his past and opened a new one into the future.[30]

You don't go into an interview with a world middleweight champion expecting to be his shrink and so, to lighten the mood, I asked him his opinion of Marvin Hagler, who had just been crowned World Middleweight Champion. "He's pretty good," the Champ joked, "but he better not get in the ring with me."

Brock Peters and I were winding down a day of press appearances; I can't remember the name of the film, but his many previous roles included Tom Robinson in *To Kill a Mockingbird*, Stephen Kumalo in *Lost in the Stars*, and a powerful Crown in *Porgy and Bess*. As we rode up to his suite in the Sheraton-Boston Towers he was humming something to himself that I faintly recognized. It was driving me crazy so I finally had to ask. "*Last Tango in Paris*," he said quietly in his rumbling *basso profundo*. I don't know why this sticks in my mind, but the man had phenomenal presence.

So did Sonny Grosso, the former New York City detective who, with his partner Eddie Egan, broke the infamous French Connection case that was turned into William Friedkin's Oscar-winning 1971 film. Seeing the opportunity, Sonny moved into film and TV producing after playing small roles in *The French Connection* and *The Godfather* ("He's clean, Captain. The kid's a war hero"). With his producing partner Larry Ja-

---

30 In 2012 director Martin Guigui filmed *Raging Bull II* which extended the LaMotta story and filled in many blanks with a stunning performance by William Forsythe. MGM, which by then owned *Raging Bull*, claimed infringement and *Raging Bull II* became *The Bronx Bull*. It had a furtive release in 2017.

cobson, Sonny executive-produced Gayle Kirschenbaum's and my HBO documentary *Judgment Day* (2003).

Hanging around Sonny was an experience in observing the use of power. First, once a cop, always a cop, and I never felt safer in my life. Second, he packed. Third, his stories were formidable and his love for Eddie Egan was inspirational. When Eddie died and the NYPD wanted to blow off his funeral, Sonny arranged for a hero's burial. He told great stories and didn't take shit from anyone. But there were still lines you couldn't cross; to this day I don't know where he lives or anything about his personal life. One night during a break from production we walked a few blocks up from what were then the Third Avenue offices of Grosso-Jacobson Productions "to get some macaroni." This was Sonny's way of extending a dinner invitation. (I also got to sit at his Monday night table at Rao's, but that's another story.) We walked into an Italian restaurant where he was known. It had to be a good restaurant because there was a picture of Frank Sinatra on the wall. Before we got seated, Sonny walked over to another table where four friends of his were having dinner. I knew enough about protocol not to join him without being invited as well as not to sit down at his table before he did. So I stood there looking at the picture of Sinatra. Soon Sonny said goodbye to his friends and we sat down with Sonny making sure to keep his back to the wall. We talked about some of his past cases and, somewhere between the antipasto and the dolce, I asked, "Hey, Sonny, do you ever bump into anybody you sent up?"

"Yeah," he said, "those guys," and nodded to the foursome I thought were his friends. "They're made guys and they're not supposed to be hanging around together or they can all get sent back to the pen. But I'm not working tonight. Want an espresso?"

The man who broke Sonny into the business was William Friedkin, whom everybody calls Billy. Billy also broke me into the book business, allowing me to write his biography (*Hurricane Billy*, NY: William Morrow, 1990). Friedkin is as mercurial and forthright as his films, which ranged, as I have noted, from *The French Connection* and *The Exorcist* to *To Live and Die in LA* and *Sorcerer*. Of the many hours I've spent with him over the decades, one stands out that has nothing to do with filmmaking, but it's still in character. I was visiting him in Montreal where he was shooting *The C.A.T. Squad* for NBC while waiting for a theatrical feature to come together. He made tea at his location apartment. While we talked idly about life, he filled the kettle, boiled the water, warmed the pot, spooned loose tea into it, covered the steeping teapot with a cozy, got the milk, and then strained and served the brew. All right, anybody can make tea, and everybody can also hold a conversation while doing it. But the image of the man who once slugged a priest to get a performance out of him delicately adding milk and sugar to a china teacup tops forty years of other moments. Apparently it impressed Randy Jorgensen, too. Randy is a former undercover cop (*Cruising*) who has made pictures with Friedkin and produced a few on his own. "What amazes me about Billy," he told me, "is how he can cook breakfast and have everything come out all at the same time and be perfectly done, too."

It's the little things about big people that make them human.

Toga! Toga! Toga!

WE KNEW *Animal House* was going to be a hit before the studio did. When I say "we," I mean the 800 radio station contest winners and the movie critics who packed the Sack Cheri Cinema in June of 1978, a month before the Universal Pictures comedy was scheduled to open in the college town of Boston. No one knew what to expect except that the film sprung from the guys at the *National Lampoon*, the bewitchingly sick humor magazine that itself had been whelped from the *Harvard Lampoon* and shared genes with NBC's *Saturday Night Live* which had debuted in 1975.

With that pedigree, magazine editor Geoffrey Precourt, writer Jib Ellis, and I took our seats, endured the T-shirts and patter offered by the hosting DJ, and started laughing thirty seconds into the show when Tom Hulce and Stephen Furst passed a statue of the founder of Faber College with the quote, "Knowledge is Good" written on its base. The rest is history.

Animal House is one of the most subversive movies ever made. It had its origins in the twisted minds of Doug Kenney, Chris Miller, and Harold Ramis, three mainstays of the *National Lampoon* who correctly figured that their college experiences in the 1960s would find resonance with kids everywhere. No shit, Shakespeare. In fact, even kids who never went to college (such as the film's director, John Landis) bonded with its gentle anarchism. Set in September of 1962—before the Cuban Missile Crisis of October, 1962, the JFK assassination of November, 1963, and the expansion of the war in Vietnam—the film is, in large sense, about

America's transition between the repressed 50s and the social upheavals of the 60s.

Enough has been written about *Animal House* that it would be silly to rehash it here, but I have a backstory that may shed some light on its creation. Some time in 1971 I was invited to dinner at Boston University's George Sherman Union by Ken Rogoff, who ran the university's Distinguished Lecture Series (he had set up the highly successful Charlton Heston appearance in October of 1970 when I was promoting Heston's *Julius Caesar*). BU was not known for its cuisine, but we were assured that its private dining facility met higher standards. The dinner was being held for that night's speaker, Doug Kenney, whom everybody at the table knew from the 'Poon and its broadcasting gambit, *The National Lampoon Radio Hour*. With little effort, the dinner devolved into both a discussion and a display of college humor. At some point Doug whipped out a fair-sized spliff, set fire to it, passed it around, and Bob's your stoned Uncle. After that, we floated into the lecture venue, Hayden Hall.

It doesn't take a lot of imagination to predict how Kenney's lecture went after that. Right from the start it veered off the rails when somebody ran up from the audience with a pie and let him have it right in the kisser. His eyeglasses saved him from being blinded but the goo that didn't hit his face flew onto Hayden Hall's plush curtains. (The cleaning bill would eat up the lecture's box office receipts.)

Kenney's comments were, at best, free-form. He spent a great deal of time talking about how teenage Communists from outer space were invading earth, and how you could always tell who they were because they opened up Mexican food stands with a big TACOS sign on top, which of course stands for Teen Age Commies from Outer Space. The night was a success for those of us who attended, and the rest caught up later once Kenney joined forces with Chris Miller and Harold Ramis to write *Animal House* based on an aborted memoir that Miller had written about his ribald experiences at Dartmouth.

Having seen and loved *Animal House*, having radio shows on both WITS-AM and WEEI-FM, and having a cordial relationship with Universal Pictures, I was asked if I wanted to have drinks with Chris Miller, Jamie Widdoes (Delta House President Robert Hoover), and Karen Allen (Katie) when they came to town on press tour. Rather than challenge the propriety of the Ritz-Carlton, we gathered in a South End restaurant.

A hit movie makes it own gravy. Just as audiences somehow know a good picture from a stinker before its premiere, interviewers and celebrities share the experience of not having to lie or be defensive. Karen, Chris, Jamie, and I had a ball talking about our college adventures, sometimes using excessively precise descriptions. After intense editing, I aired as much of the interview as the FCC would allow.[31]

"Do you remember the Eliot Lounge?" Miller asked. "We used to come down here from Dartmouth to get drunk in the Eliot Lounge." The Eliot Lounge was in the Eliot Hotel, 370 Commonwealth Avenue in Boston's sedate Back Bay. "They had whiskey sours two for a dollar. They called it 'The Sour Hour.' We'd drink there and then drive through Kenmore Square throwing moons."

"Come on," said Widdoes, "Karen's here."

"One time we had six of us in a car," Miller continued, ignoring her. "And we threw a sextuple moon. We had guys on both sides that dropped trou, a guy in front with the window open, the driver was throwing an elephant, and in the back we had a pressed ham against the window."

"That's only five," I said.

---

31 NOTE: While this section was being written, the Presidential campaign of 2016 was in full implosion and Republican candidate Donald Trump's offensive locker room comments came to light. Not that they were much different from the other offensive things he had been saying all along, but his casual attitude toward sexual assaulting women became the tipping point. Media outlets—who had been hypocritically encouraging and covering him all along—were suddenly faced with how to report the specifics of his vulgar language. Naturally they ran it all, allowing themselves to pander to the prurient interests of their audience while appearing to chastise the man who said them. In light of this, I considered cutting this section because it appeared to veer close to the behavior that swept Trump into the White House. But it's different, and I'll tell you why. Yes, the characters in *Animal House* spoke the locker room banter that people criticized in Trump, but they did so with a juvenile innocence and never acted on them. Moreover, they are presented in the context of the early 1960s before enlightenment. At the same time, the filmmakers framed the material from the perspective of the late 1970s to make a point. The ogres in *Animal House* are not the crass Deltas, they are the evil Omegas: Dougie, Greggie, "and the rest of the Hitler Youth." The Omegas' crime is not that they are killjoys but that they will soon bend the world to their selfish, sexist, racist, bellicose views. Who'd-a thunk that *Animal House* would predict the future with such accuracy?

"Okay, but one of 'em got turned into a double hog back growler."

"What's a double hog back growler?" Allen asked.

"Oh, Chris, really, this is so gross," Widdoes insisted.

"Don't worry," Allen said, "I've seen every part of the male anatomy."

Miller took the cue. "You take everything and push it back between your legs," he said. (Sometimes you just have to sit back and marvel at the way a guy who really knows his stuff can explain it like he's doing a simple math problem.) "And you spread your cheeks and fart. The fart is the growl."

"I must admit I've never heard of pressed hams or a double hog back growler," I confessed. "And I went to college."

"Yeah, but were you in a fraternity?" Widdoes asked.

"No," I said, "we kicked them off campus along with ROTC."

"Then I guess you never heard of a wind tunnel," Miller said between sips of beer.

I hadn't.

"Karen, do you mind?" he condescended. She shook her head no.

"I won't be too specific," he said, "but only girls can do it."

"The National Lampoon was famous for off-color humor," I said. "In fact, I'd have to call it sick, like 'Hire the Handicapped' and other features in truly bad taste. Did you have any limits?"

"Yes," Miller said, surprising me by becoming serious. "In fact, we had a rule. It isn't enough that a joke is in bad taste, it also has to be funny." Believe it or not, I've used that wisdom ever since.

The Saturday after *Animal House* opened, Geoffrey Precourt, Jib Ellis, and I took over WITS-AM for my "Behind the Scenes" show, played back a carefully edited tape of the Miller-Widdoes-Allen interview, and threw our own toga party in Studio A. We celebrated our college adventures, urged listeners to see *Animal House*, and frankly didn't care how many people could hear us. The film, which cost $2.6 million to make, went on to gross, at last count, $141 million, making it one of the most profitable pictures in Hollywood history. It catapulted director John Landis into the forefront of comedy filmmakers and made a star out of John Belushi.

I met Landis when he was coming through town to promote *The Blues Brothers*, his follow-up to *Animal House*. We had been pre-introduced by

Saul Kahan, a publicist who had worked with Landis on his debut film *Schlock* (1973) and whom I had met when he was unit publicist on *The Friends of Eddie Coyle* (1973). At the time of *Blues Brothers* Landis was 28 and fulminating with excitement. It was as if everything he said ended with an exclamation point. A Hollywood kid, he had entered filmmaking at 18 as a crew member on *Kelly's Heroes* (1970) as the protégé of Andrew Marton, one of the finest action directors in the business.

What distinguishes Landis is not just his exuberance but also his style, both personal and cinematic. He invariably dresses in jacket and tie, is devoted to film history and the tradition of his craft, and is perhaps the finest comedy director since Blake Edwards. I'm not referring only to his sense of timing and his blocking of scenes, I also mean his camera placement that focuses the viewer's attention without the appearance of artifice. The man knows how to set up and pull off gags both physical and verbal.

It is a horrible irony that someone so good at what he does will forever be tarred by the terrible events of July 23, 1982. That is the night that Vic Morrow, Mica Dinh Le, and Renee Shin-Yi Chen were killed when a pyrotechnic effect went terribly wrong on the set of *The Twilight Zone: The Movie*. In a sequence set during the Vietnam War, Morrow and the children were crossing a bog when helicopters overhead exploded and fell on them. Six copter passengers were also injured. A trial, years of speculation, and two books probed how such a thing could happen and, more accusingly, how much Landis, Executive Producer Steven Spielberg, and Producers Frank Marshall and George Folsey, Jr. had been involved in allowing under-age children to be present near explosives or, for that matter, to be working after dark, period. Landis was criticized for recklessness in ordering the copters to get nearer to the actors.

I wasn't there, nor have I spoken to anybody who was, but I do know a lot of people who work on film crews and I have a take on what happened. I see the accident as the result of not only several small wrong decisions combining into one deadly event but of Hollywood protocol. Here is John Landis calling for a more thrilling scene. Here are crew members working on a major studio film (Warner Bros.). Here is a director whose last four films (*Animal House, Blues Brothers, An American Werewolf in London, Trading Places*) grossed in excess of $377 million dollars. Who is going to risk his career saying, "Um, Mr. Landis, this is dangerous and I don't think we should be doing it"? In a business where only the director is allowed to say "cut," what status does a single crew member have? In other words, it wasn't malicious and it didn't have to happen, but it did.

Since then, the movie industry has instituted safety measures and far tighter restrictions on child actors.[32] CGI technology and detailed miniatures have also reduced the need for, and therefore the risk of, live explosions. But there were still three deaths on *The Twilight Zone*. Four, counting the movie.

And there was another death. Doug Kenney, who, after *Animal House*, co-scripted *Caddy Shack* (1980), did not live to enjoy what would have been a long career. On August 27, 1980 he was sightseeing in Kauai, Hawaii when the lip of the cliff he was standing on crumbled. He died in the fall.

"We went to his funeral," Tom Davis, Al Franken's comedy partner (Franken and Davis), told me afterward. "It was bizarre. The preacher, in his eulogy, talked about how death was like leaves falling from a tree onto the ground, and I thought how he didn't seem to grasp the image that Doug had fallen to his death from a very high cliff." On the other hand, I like to think that Kenney would have appreciated the dark humor.

John Landis and I had another exchange when I produced the John Belushi *Biography* for A&E Networks. It's minor, but I take pleasure from it. "There's something that I wanted to ask you about the released version of your film," I said. "It's a scene right after Belushi stuffs his face with food in the cafeteria line before he carries his tray into the lunchroom. But first, at the end of the line, he has a tug-of-war with a cafeteria worker—"

"That's me," Landis interjected. "I shaved off my beard and everything."

"—and yanks the tray back from the worker's hands making him tumble over a stack of glassware, saying, 'If you want to fuck with the eagles, you better know how to fly.'"

"We cut that out of the film," Landis said.

---

32 Injuries and deaths on movie sets are more frequent than the public thinks but seldom receive wide press coverage. One that did was the 2014 death of second camera assistant Sarah Jones who was killed on the set of *Midnight Rider: The Gregg Allman Story* when she was hit by a train during an unauthorized set-up on a railroad trestle. Again the film industry called for safer working conditions.

"I saw it."

"You couldn't have."

"I saw it in the film or I wouldn't be able to quote it to you. But it's not in the home video."

"It's in the photo book we made of the movie," Landis insisted. "You probably saw it there and thought you saw it in the movie."

But I did see it. It was in the preview print that Universal provided for the Boston radio promotional screening. I wonder what happened to it. Is it still in the studio's vault or did they ship it to some anonymous regional theatre to fulfill an engagement and accidentally send them the uncut *Animal House*? Or did it find its way into a collector's closet awaiting discovery?

The immense success of *Animal House*, not surprisingly, created a whole new genre in screen comedy: gross-out pictures, the ultimate of which are films like *The Hangover* (2009) and *Bridesmaids* (2011). They're funny but they don't have the heart, wit, or innocence of the one that started it all.

Or maybe didn't start it all. In 1961, independent New York filmmaker Robert Downey, Sr. had begun writing and directing a string of iconoclastic short comedies with such challenging titles as "Ball's Bluff," "Babo 73," "Chafed Elbows," and "No More Excuses." His warm demeanor despite a rapier-like sense of humor earned him the appellation "a prince" which he appended to his directing credit for years—e.g., "Directed by Robert Downey (a prince)." Where other filmmakers in the New Cinema movement of the 50s and 60s seemed more concerned with politics, sex, conformity, or ennui, Downey threw them into a cinematic blender. His early works played mainly in film societies to the coffee house set. In 1969, however, he achieved crossover success with *Putney Swope*, a satire about a black man who takes control of a Madison Avenue advertising agency and proves that the public will buy more products if they're told the truth about them. Downey made several more pointed, offbeat pictures such as the Christ parable *Greaser's Palace* and *Pound*, a truly unclassifiable satire with humans playing dogs. He hit a major snag in 1980, however, when he had a falling out with Warner Bros. over *Up the Academy*, a dismal attempt by *Mad Magazine* to blend *Animal House* and *Police Academy*. Apparently Downey's off-the-wall humor was too off-the-wall for a major studio and he returned to independent filmmaking and directing the occasional TV episode. To date his most successful production remains Robert Downey, Jr.

There is a coda to this story. Over breakfast, Downey told me that some time in the 1980s he was taking a pitch meeting with an executive at Universal. He was too discrete to name him (that alone was remarkable) but I got the sense it was Sean Daniel, the enormously successful producer who had been at Universal when *Animal House* was made. "We owe you a debt of gratitude," the exec told Downey. "If you hadn't made all those pictures in the 1960s, we never could have gotten away with making *Animal House*. Yes sir, we owe you a big debt." Downey thanked him and said, in response, "So how about paying it back?"

In five minutes, the meeting was over.

John Landis doesn't make many films any more, either. He shifted to documentaries like *The Slasher* (2004) about a super car salesman and *Mr. Warmth: The Don Rickles Project* (2007). In 2010 he directed *Burke and Hare* about Britain's notorious body snatchers and has executive produced numerous TV and feature projects. But the director of *Animal House*, *Trading Places*, *Coming to America* and Michael Jackson's *Thriller* still has plenty of pictures in him. Just ask Babs.[33]

Landis and Downey both know how to fly with the eagles. Trouble is, Hollywood raises pigeons.

---

33 Landis fans will recognize Babs as Babs Jansen, the character played by Martha Smith in *Animal House*, who becomes a tour guide at Universal City Studios in the film's "where are they now" end sequence. Universal routinely put a card on the end of all their releases saying, "When in Southern California visit Universal City Studios." Whenever Landis made a movie for them, he always added "ask for Babs." I realize I've just spent a whole paragraph explaining a three-word joke. If you're reading this now it's because my editor liked it. (P.S.: He said he did.)

Lost in New York

"THE FIRST THING you'll see when you step outside of LAX are the palm trees," Russell Manker said. "And it gets better from there." Russ, who had brought me into the TV game with *Evening Magazine*, had relocated to Los Angeles to work for Woody Fraser, the visionary producer for Group W Productions who had taken *The Mike Douglas Show* from a Westinghouse station in Philadelphia to national syndication and then turned to producing one of the first reality shows, *That's Incredible!* I was visiting Russ in 1981 on the tail end of a now-forgotten press junket. He was oddly positive about the city, having forsaken the comforting intelligence of Boston for the warmth—we're talking weather, not attitude—of Hollywood. He had an apartment in a small building in West Hollywood, one of the neighborhoods that's actually a neighborhood and not connecting tissue between freeway exits. We went to an outdoor cafe, had salads (wherein I tasted my first tomato that actually tasted like a tomato and not a golf ball painted red) and watched the migration of wannabes on Santa Monica Boulevard. The city still allowed public smoking in those days, and Russ and I took perverse pleasure in directing each other's attention to the male and female models carrying their portfolios in one hand and a lit cigarette in the other. "Look at them," he said. "They eat health food, they go to the gym every day to keep in shape, and what do they do? They smoke."

Not that you could tell the difference in the air. "I'm not sure about the palm trees," I told Russ over coffee, "but I'll tell you the first thing I noticed when the plane cleared the mountains and made the approach to

LAX. The air was brown. It was like someone had taken the skyline and wiped their ass with it."

"Yep," he said." Welcome to LA."

LA's air used to be as bad as New York's. People made smog jokes[34] but it wasn't funny, and it was only as the new century began that the cynics had to agree that the environmental laws that the lobbyists had complained about made a healthful difference.

This wasn't the first time I had visited the city. I had been flown there in early 1975 by Twentieth Century-Fox, not for a press junket but for a meeting to go over the studio's upcoming releases, for I had just been hired as an assistant advertising-publicity man in their New York office. The film I had helped to publicize the year before, *The Towering Inferno*, had been a huge success and therefore, by Hollywood logic, anybody who was connected with it even in the smallest way basked in the credit. (It also works in the other direction; if you have the most marginal connection with a flop, even your imaginary friend won't return your phone calls.)

I had never been to either Los Angeles or a studio before and Fox was a fine place to start. It boasted the best landscaping of all the old time dream factories and, they assured us as we entered the commissary, the best food. We were not to have this confirmed, as it was a morning meeting and they kicked us out before the lunch bell. Everyone was in fine spirits. Both *The Towering Inferno* and *Young Frankenstein* were still pulling in bucks, and Mel Brooks stopped by for a few minutes to give us a pep talk. I have no memory of what he said, but it was very funny and very Jewish. I wondered if he knew we were attaching every expense we could think of to his picture even if they weren't his.

Johnny Friedkin (no relation to director William Friedkin) was running the studio's publicity. He was not only as sharp as they come, but he taught me a lesson in corporate grammar that I have never forgotten. I call it "third person innocent" and it happened during this very meeting. Johnny was going over the campaign for some upcoming Fox release when a terrible metallic crash sounded from the kitchen. Then silence. Johnny said, "A meatball was just dropped," and everybody laughed. The line wasn't that funny—my own mother used to explain such noises by saying, "I dropped my teeth,"—but the brilliance lay in his use of the pas-

---

34 "Knock knock." "Who's there?" "UCLA." "UCLA who?" "You see LA when the smog lifts." I think that one was from Stan Freberg.

sive voice. Obviously meatballs don't drop themselves. Somebody had to have done it. But by using third person innocent—"A meatball was just dropped"—he avoided ascribing blame to anyone and a corporate culpability crisis was deftly avoided.

I was summoned back to the studio that night to visit David Forbes, the young marketing whiz who had liberated me from Sack Theatres a few months earlier. The studio was so cramped for space that they had put David and his small overworked staff in a construction trailer behind one of the sound stages. He should have had an office by now but—and this is another tidbit of Hollywood protocol—they were holding it up because he wanted to move in without having it redecorated. Ordinarily, executives are allowed to have their new offices re-carpeted and re-painted, then they go to the studio's massive collection of set dressings to choose furniture. This is how Richard D. Zanuck came across his late father's (Darryl F. Zanuck) famous desk—the one that DFZ supposedly used every afternoon to have sex with one of the contract starlets—and made it his own. (When I interviewed him for the A&E *Biography* on his father, I surreptitiously checked it for fingernail, heel, and zipper marks. Nada.)

David would have none of this. He just wanted to move in and do his job[35] but his higher-ups couldn't understand why. After all, if he wouldn't upgrade his digs, , how could they justify their own expensive redecorating? Not only that, David insisted on his company car being a Jeep. This was before SUVs became all the rage. Fox leaned on him to get a Mercedes. Eventually the leaning failed and David drove his Jeep onto the lot and worked in his new office with the old furnishings.

A movie studio is a dream factory because when it goes to sleep at night it turns off the lights. On this moonless night as I left David's trailer, I not only didn't know that you can't hail a cab in Los Angeles, I couldn't find the front gate and ask the guard to call one. I got lost on the studio's back lot. Rows of tenement buildings blocked me from finding the administration building. The other direction was the Fox theatre where founder William Fox had screened his first Movietone newsreels. Reversing direction, I hit the small town square where George C. Scott and Michael Sarrazin had been called to justice in *The Flim-Flam Man*. The sidewalks were abnormally high and I reasoned that this was so the

---

35 A job, by the way, that would soon revolutionize movie marketing. See the Author's *Stirling Silliphant: The Fingers of God*.

production designer could lay a variety of street surfaces (asphalt, dirt, cobblestone, etc.) to bring them up to normal height for filming. There were streetlights in front of the brownstones but, of course, they weren't real. Only the moon lit my way, and badly. I was starting to panic. To hell with fantasy, I wanted to get back to my hotel. Suddenly I saw cobblestones. They started out of nowhere and led me around a bend. Suddenly I was in New York City, 1890, smack in the middle of the *Hello Dolly* street. Between the plywood mailboxes, storefront façades, and elevated railroad (built in perspective), I expected Barbra Streisand to step off a horse-drawn cart and hand me a business card for Dolly Levi. After *Hello Dolly* was finished in 1969 (and after *Hello Dolly* nearly finished Fox), the studio kept the opulent set standing, presumably as a reminder against ever making another big-budget musical. In 1976 director Mark Rydell used it for his screwy buddy picture *Harry and Walter Go to New York* (a personal favorite) but the *Hello Dolly* curse settled upon that effort as well, and when Rupert Murdoch bought the studio in 1984 it was one of the first things to go. By then I had escaped from publicity and had become a critic.

Visiting the studios as a critic is far different from going as an employee. They put on a show for you. When I was an entertainment reporter with a background as a studio worker, my contact people were especially guarded. It will surprise no one to learn that Disney was the most paranoid. When I was flown out to Disneyland with over a hundred other reporters for a junket to mark the park's 40th anniversary, we were all given free run of the place, no E-tickets to worry about, and we could cut in line for the rides (note: not recommended). The joy was dulled, however, because each of us was accompanied by a Disney employee. The company was heavy with publicists, but by the time they got to the "S's" for "Segaloff" they had run out and I found myself attached to a smiling, red-headed lad who played Prince Charming in the *Cinderella* parade that pranced through the park at sundown. (I won't name him because the Disney folks never forget.) Fittingly, he was dating the young woman who played Cinderella.

I couldn't shake him. "Let's go see Country Bear Jamboree," I said, hoping to bore him into leaving me alone. Instead, he chirped, "Hey, what a good idea. I haven't seen that in a long time." The show consisted of Audio Animatronic® figures moving to playback of a show so corny it could have been written with niblets. Prince Charming told me that it had been programmed by Marc Davis, one of Walt's original "nine old men" who perfected the art of screen animation. Knowing this made me appreciate what I—make that we—were watching.

Still unable to peel him from my side, I figured I could lose him in the men's room. Instead, he waited for me outside like a dutiful puppy. I was about to dare him to go through "It's a Small World" with me when I noticed that the asphalt between the trolley tracks on Main Street, USA was softer than the pavement outside the tracks. "That's on purpose," my escort said. "We make it that way so the horses don't hurt their hooves when they pull the carts." Figuring that there might be some more tidbits I could weave into a story, I mentioned that the bus that carried my fellow reporters and me to the park that morning had taken a wrong turn and had brought us in through the underground network of passages known as "backstage." "Oooh, that's too bad for the driver," the prince moaned. "Outsiders aren't supposed to see that. I hope the driver doesn't get fired."

"For driving us backstage?"

"The press? Are you kidding? It's off limits."

He wouldn't elaborate, even when I told him I had done publicity for Disney. Apparently the studio and the park are separated by a great gulf. So I punted. I hardly ever do this, but I figured, okay, here's Prince Charming, let's try the only Cinderella joke I knew.

"Do you know how Cinderella died?" I asked.

"How?" Prince Charming said guilelessly.

"At midnight her tampon turned into a pumpkin."

There was that uncomfortable beat where he didn't know whether to laugh and I didn't know whether to apologize. He laughed.

"Okay, okay," he said, loosening up. "Let's have some dish."

We spent the next hour walking all over the park, off the record, having a great time. Trust me, he was no longer bland, he was as sharp as they come. I learned about a stabbing that had taken place in the Magic Kingdom where, in order to avoid publicity, Disney Security had driven the victim to the nearest hospital rather than call an ambulance, but because the car had to stop for red lights, the guest bled to death. I learned that undercover security people are stationed throughout the park to guard against child molesters, that people suspected of shoplifting are sequestered in private rooms until they confess, and that not everybody caught smoking pot is banned for life. I also learned that the head of security, behind his back, was called Mr. Potatohead. (NOTE: I have no way of knowing which, if any, of these are true, but I'm including them to show what an efficient organization Disney was even before it took over ABC and became a media conglomerate.)

The Disney Studio itself also has tight security, but there was less of it the first time I visited. Talking with a friend outside the commissary after lunch, I felt something tugging on my trouser leg. It was a chipmunk begging for food. Talk about cheeky. All I could think of to tell my friend was, "Gosh you make them look so lifelike here." Not to be beaten, he said, "Oh, that's Chip. He hasn't been the same since Dale broke up the act."

Just as the films produced by the classic Hollywood studios had individual styles, so did the physical plants. Alas, I was born too late to visit them while their founding moguls were still running them. The closest I came was having lunch in the MGM commissary when I was distracted midway through a bowl of Louis B. Mayer's mother's chicken matzo ball soup as David Begelman entered. Begelman had been hired to run MGM after he was forced out of Columbia Pictures by stockholder and public pressure for forging checks. The publicist I was having lunch with pointed him out to me. He was wearing a shiny dark green suit that I thought didn't fit him very well, and all I could think of to say to my companion was, "Good god, he looks like Nixon."

My only other mogul sighting was the genuine article. Hurrying to a meeting at Universal Pictures, I rounded a soundstage and suddenly faced Lew Wasserman, the legendary power broker who turned Universal into an industry leader. Tall, rail thin, white-haired, and with pale skin that made his outsized tinted eyeglasses seem even larger and darker, he returned my shocked stare with patrician indifference. I made it to my meeting, which was a fruitless effort to license film clips of Rocky and Bullwinkle to make an A&E *Biography* about their creator, Jay Ward. Ward's widow and daughter supported the idea and so did Universal, which had purchased the character rights from them, but the Saatchi & Saatchi advertising agency, which owned the original *Rocky and His Friends* TV series made by General Mills Cereals, wouldn't budge. They wanted what amounted to our entire budget for just ten minutes of footage. The *Biography* was going to be a contrivance anyway because the late Jay Ward had been obsessively publicity shy and I had designed his episode to be a search for him ala *Citizen Kane*. When it was clear that the project was doomed, I resorted to the kind of Hail Mary play I had tried with Prince Charming. "So tell me," I asked the Universal Pictures merchandising people. "How are the *Schindler's List* action figures doing?"

Russ Manker was right. The first thing you see in LA are the palm trees. But it's the rest of the stuff you remember.

Nuggets

GERTRUDE STEIN may have said, "You know what you know, you know?" but she didn't get out of the house much.[36] Those whose lives or jobs or both bring them into contact with a variety of people learn more than if they had stayed in one town, or with one circle of friends, or even in a house at 27 rue de Fleurus. This is why reporters become encyclopedic. As Sherman Reilly Duffy, City Editor of the *Chicago Journal*, told fledgling scribe Ben Hecht (who later quoted him in *A Child of the Century*), "Socially a journalist fits in somewhere between a whore and a bartender, but spiritually he stands beside Galileo. He knows the world is round."

Not everybody in Hollywood makes movies, but the best of those who do bring life experiences to their screen work. This is why so many modern films that are made by people whose life experience is only movies, TV, and comics are lacking in human empathy or, hell, human interest. There ought to be a law that says you have to live life before you make movies.

Tony Giorgio, who had been a professional pickpocket before trying his hand at acting, never quite left his first profession behind, although he shifted to practicing it on the side of law enforcement. He was visiting Boston with Bruce Geller, the writer-producer not only of *Mission:*

---

36 What Stein actually said—rather, wrote—was, "Do you know because I tell you so, or do you know, do you know?" (Libretto for the opera *The Mother Of Us All* by Virgil Thomson, 1947) but this rewrite, which I got from James Bridges, is too good to pass up.)

Impossible but of Georgio's new film, *Harry In Your Pocket*. Tony knew his stuff. "Never keep your wallet in your back pants pocket if you're in a crowd," he urged over dinner. "That's where you'll get it picked. Put it in your thigh pocket. And never use a money clip; always keep your bills loose. If you use a money clip, it all comes out at once if you get your pocket picked."

"Yeah, but why the thigh pocket?" Geller asked.

"Because it's right near your balls," Giorgio said, "and no pickpocket is going to reach for your balls just to make a few bucks." He also said that pickpockets will work together in a group of bystanders at a concert or circus. Someone will yell out, "Watch out! There's a pickpocket in this crowd," and every guy will reach for his wallet to check on it, thereby showing every pickpocket exactly where he keeps his money.

Another piece of wisdom came from Amarillo Slim, whom Columbia sent on tour to talk about *California Split*, the Robert Altman movie he'd just made with Elliott Gould and George Segal. Between card tricks, the colorful Slim reminded the press of the ageless wisdom, "Never eat at a restaurant named Mom's, never sit down to play poker with anybody named after a city (he smiled at himself), and never, even if you disregard the other two, go to bed with anyone whose troubles are worse than yours." As he dealt hands to everyone at the table he also said, "If you sit down to play poker, look around the table, and if you can't tell who the sucker is, it's you."

* * *

The waiter at Boston's ever-so-proper Ritz-Carlton hotel placed Charlton Heston's luncheon plate before him. The menu was lamb chops, and—formal service being what it was—the chef had placed ruffled "panties" on the bone ends. While the reporters interviewing him cut theirs with knife and fork, Heston picked up the chops with his fingers and took a bite. Having written *The Everything® Etiquette Book* I can tell you that, technically, he was correct; one may use the fingers to eat food if it has bones but no sauce (fried chicken yes, chicken fricassee no) and especially if the bone is covered. But it did create a tense silence until everyone realized, hey, if Moses can do it, why not? (No one copied him anyway.)

* * *

The best advice I ever got from a newspaper was from Terry Byrne, the assistant Arts Editor at *The Boston Herald*. I had made some kind of minor mistake in a story I had written—used the wrong first name in a credit or something—and I figured, since it wasn't life-threatening. I'd apologize. "Are you out of your mind?" Terry said, stopping me. "Never apologize for anything!"

"Why not?" I asked. "It isn't a big thing."

"Maybe not to you, but there will be another edition of the paper tomorrow and by then nobody will remember your mistake. All that anybody around here will remember is that you were the idiot who apologized for something."

* * *

"Film schools aren't training directors," writer-director James Bridges lamented, "They're training second unit directors." Second unit directors are responsible for staging the action scenes in movies. "They know where to put the camera, they know all about cutting, and they make a dynamic film, but they don't know how to talk to actors. That's why so many films today lack the human element." To address this problem, Bridges and his partner Jack Larson established the James Bridges Award in Film Directing yearly at UCLA, USC, Columbia, and the American Film Institute to encourage directors to take acting classes so they know how to communicate with the humans in their films and not just the cameras.

* * *

"A novel, to be a novel, must be novel." Gregory Mcdonald knew what he was talking about. His *Fletch*, *Flynn*, and *Skyler* mysteries were all bestsellers and he used them to bend the genre without his readers noticing the stretch marks. "Mystery novels tend to be written by Liberals and appeal mostly to Conservatives," he once explained. "Liberals like them because they point out all the problems with the System, such as when you pick up a telephone in an emergency and it doesn't work. And Conservatives like them because everything comes out okay in the end, which shows that the system does, in fact, work."

Mcdonald, whose penchant for privacy bordered on an obsession, ventured into the public eye whenever he had to publicize a new title, after which he retreated to his farm in a rural southern town. "Of course I call it old Mcdonald's farm," he joked. As a testament to how well he was respected there, his neighbors adopted the habit of deflecting curious fans by sending them in the opposite direction. Greg had the ability to hold an entire mystery plot in his head until he was ready to write it, and then he sat down at the computer and went from start to finish as fast as he could type. "Writing a novel is easy," he joked, but even his joke made sense the more you think about it. "In the beginning you tell a lie, and by the end you tell a truth." Greg's life—I knew him for four decades of it—was all truth, and that's no lie.

* * *

"So you're the guys who killed Bambi's mother!"

Frank Thomas and Ollie Johnston had heard it before, but this was the first time they'd gotten it from me, and I was only half-kidding. The first time I saw *Bambi* was with my Aunt Helen at a reissue at RKO Keith's in Washington, DC, and the beauty of the film was ruined by some little kid whining, all during the second half, "Mommy, what happened to Bambi's mother?" So this encounter was personal.

Frank and Ollie—two of Disney's famous "nine old men"—were granting me an interview on the occasion of the film's reissue and had invited me to pay them a home visit. The Johnstons and the Thomases lived in nearby lots in La Cañada, a gentle bedroom community east of the Disney Burbank studio. The men were close friends and collaborators and worked for Disney even before Walt took the feature plunge on *Snow White and the Seven Dwarfs*.

"We get asked that all the time," said Frank, enjoying the chance to debunk a friendly accusation. His long face and bushy eyebrows made him look like a lovable Disney character. "But if you read Felix Salten's book, all it says is that Bambi's mother tells him to run for the thicket, a shot rings out, and it says, 'Bambi never saw his mother again.' Our job was to make those words play dramatically."

It's true: from *Bambi: A Life in the Woods*:

> "There weren't any tracks," said Aunt Ena. "But . . . His . . . tracks were there. He found Gobo."
>
> She was silent. Then Bambi asked despondently, "Aunt Ena, have you seen my mother?"
>
> "No," answered Aunt Ena gently.
>
> Bambi never saw his mother again.[37]

---

37 ©1926 Paul Zsolnay Verlag; renewed 1954 by Anna Wyler Salten; English language translation ©1928 by Simon & Schuster; renewed 1956 Simon & Schuster, Inc.

As Ollie and Frank wrote in their 1990 book *Bambi, The Story and the Film*, "We settled on the two of them running as fast as they could, with the mother calling, 'Don't look back!' They come to a log lying over the path and Bambi darts underneath. The mother leaps over the log, going out of frame, and at that moment the shot is heard. . . ."[38] Disney was meticulous about keeping story conference notes, and these go on to refine how the mother's death protecting Bambi in a blizzard is to be presented. At one point the audience was even going to see her body's imprint in the snow.

There is no way to adequately describe my feeling of sitting with people like Frank Thomas and Ollie Johnston, or, at other times, with the great animation artists Marc Davis, Woolie Reitherman, Ken Anderson, Ward Kimball, Eyvind Earle, and Art Stevens, among others whom the Disney people made available to the press on special occasions. After years of living in Walt's shadow, they finally claimed their own limelight after he died in 1966. While John Lasseter, Will Vinton, Ralph Bakshi, Caroline Leaf, and Don Bluth are major talents (and I have interviewed them too), the emotional legacy of the Disney people is part of the cultural memory of four generations of moviegoers. Just imagine what Leonard Maltin and John Canemaker—who have met them and more—must feel. I still choke up when I hear "Baby Mine" sung in *Dumbo*. I still feel joy when Tramp nudges the last meatball to Lady in *Lady and the Tramp* (a sequence that Frank Thomas drew), and I cringe when Lampwick and Pinocchio start turning into donkeys in *Pinocchio*. I know I'm being manipulated. But, damn it, my heartstrings are being tugged by line drawings, not Vivien Leigh or Lassie. Whatever monolith the Walt Disney Company may have become, the very best of their artistry is still all about wishing upon a star.

* * *

Sometimes you go after a story and sometimes a story finds you. One night shortly after the July, 1983 release of *Staying Alive*, the long-anticipated sequel to 1977's smash hit *Saturday Night Fever*, I received a call at home from the screenwriter of both films, Norman Wexler. Like everybody else, I loved *Saturday Night Fever* and, also like everybody else, I hated *Staying Alive*. In my review I couldn't understand how the superb writer of *Saturday Night Fever* (as well as *Joe* in 1970 and *Ser-*

---

38 ©The Walt Disney Corporation; NY: Stewart, Tabori & Chang, 1990.

pico in 1973, both of which nailed him Oscar nominations) could have written a sequel that not only misunderstood the vitality and importance of the original but was also so sappy and ham-fisted. Thus when Wexler identified himself I was prepared to be defensive but resolute. When he said he agreed with me, I grabbed a pen and paper.

"You do realize that you're speaking to a reporter," I said. "Yes," he responded, and started to tell me in one word what had happened to his script: "Stallone."

Wexler's tale of woe charted the changes that Sylvester Stallone, in agreeing to direct (but not appear in) the film, had made which, he assured me, were what accounted for what I saw and criticized on the screen. Wexler had been asked to write it by John Travolta only to have Stallone change it from a brittle and realistic story into something "vacuous, impoverished, crass, and crude." The original script had Tony Manero (Travolta) winding up, at best, as an anonymous chorus dancer. Instead, Stallone *Rocky*-fied both the script and its star into a buff, glitzy, overnight sensation. Not only that, Wexler insisted, he had not even been invited to a courtesy screening of the finished film and had only seen it by buying a ticket to a Connecticut movie theatre on opening day. We spoke a little while longer and, when Wexler heard that I was a writer as well as a critic, he volunteered his agent to me and said I should call him and use his name. As soon as we hung up I breathlessly called my editor at the *Boston Herald* who said, "Jesus, yes, write it."

Two days later when it ran, I eagerly phoned the agent figuring he'd praise me for showing his client such sympathy.

"Where did he call you from?" the agent asked with urgency in his voice.

"I didn't ask," I said. "I was only interested in the story."

"Look," the frazzled man said, "His family has been trying to find him. He's left home, he's gone, we don't know where. He's bipolar and he's off on a manic high."[39]

The agent and I weren't on the record so a follow-up story was out of the question, but that isn't the kind of story I'd write anyway, at least not while someone was still alive (Wexler died in 1999 at age 73). I wish

---

39 A description of his mania was written by his daughter Erica in the January 19, 2013 *London Telegraph*: (http://www.telegraph.co.uk/culture/film/9787564/The-Jekyll-and-Hyde-life-of-the-man-who-wrote-Saturday-Night-Fever.html

I'd known him in better times, although apparently even his better times were pretty wild; in 1972 he served a prison stretch after making threats against Richard Nixon while on a trans-continental flight.

Years later in Beverly Hills I saw Sylvester Stallone emerging alone from a Canon Drive cigar store that was upscale even for Beverly Hills. Sure, he'd aged, but he looked tanned, trim, fit, and every inch (though not as many as I'd expected) the movie star. For some reason I didn't ask him about *Staying Alive*. I kept walking because I don't smoke.

* * *

As everyone knows, the show business trade paper *Variety* has its own language. Much of it was invented by Sime Silverman, its founder, and added to over the decades since its first issue in 1905 by a cadre of jaded entertainment reporters who wanted to bring as much excitement to their jobs covering entertainment as the purveyors of entertainment did to audiences. Among the better-known slang, nonce, and portmanteau words found in *Variety* are boffo and socko (success at the box office), ducat (ticket), blurb (review excerpt), oater (western movie), helm (direct), mitting (applause) and chopsocky (martial arts action film). Among my personal favorites are kidvid (children's television) and the opposites freevee and feevee (broadcast television versus pay TV, which was once controversial but which everybody is now forced to have), and tub thump, a term for when a flack man (publicist) beats the PR drum to create ballyhoo (attention) for a client.

Shortly after moving to Los Angeles I came to the historic Farmer's Market at Third and Fairfax to have breakfast with Larry Jackson. Larry, as I've stated, used to run the legendary Orson Welles Cinema. While there he produced the documentary *Bugs Bunny Superstar*, the first exploration of the creative cauldron known as Termite Terrace at Warner Bros., and went on to work with Welles himself on *The Other Side of the Wind* and *Filming Othello*. Easily among the most literate of producers, Larry went on to head production for The Samuel Goldwyn Company and then Orion Pictures. When we arranged our breakfast in 1996, he had just been hired by Miramax, at the time the most successful and respected independent film company. I was excited for him as I bought my "green" (that's what you called *Daily Variety*, whose logo is in green ink) and sat down at the entrance of Farmer's Market to wait for him.

Daily Variety's front page is the bellwether for what Hollywood will talk about that day. Everyone knows the famous headline *Stix Nix Hix Pix*, meaning that small towns (the sticks) don't like (nix) movies (pix) about small towns (hicks). The other famous one is *Wall Street Lays an Egg*, noting the Great Depression in 1929. A more recent favorite announced Frank Price's dismissal as head of Universal Pictures when his studio's 1986 production of *Howard the Duck* tanked (*Duck Cooks Price's Goose*). The rest of the paper's front page may announce an important agency signing, a corporate merger, or a lawsuit. The thing that drew my attention on this morning, however, was a small item that read, "Jackson Ankles Miramax."

Ankle is *Variety*-ese for quitting ones job.

Larry had ankled, he told me as we sat down at Kokomo's Restaurant, because, after working out the terms of his new position with Harvey Weinstein, the bombastic head of Miramax, he showed up for the first day at work and the contract that was waiting for his signature didn't reflect their agreement. I didn't press Larry for details, but I did marvel, "Gee, I've never known anybody who ankled anything before." Larry has gone on to become an entrepreneur and a busy consultant for international productions. The marketing savvy that he developed as managing director of the Welles has stood him—and his clients—in good stead.

Like everything else in show business, *Variety* has become less colorful over the years, almost as if it craves respectability. So has the Farmer's Market, half of which was razed in the late 1990s to build a shopping monstrosity called The Grove, a fantasyland for upscale shoppers, enriching developers but destroying the character of the Fairfax neighborhood where I lived. Unable to appreciate the rise in traffic, noise, and congestion, I ankled the area shortly after it opened in 2002.

* * *

Gore Vidal tried to steal my pen. It was only a Bic "stic" ballpoint, the 19¢ kind with the clear shaft, and I had given it to him so he could autograph my copy of his script for the 1964 film, *The Best Man*. Years ago I had asked the film's director, Franklin J. Schaffner, to sign it. The setting was the 2010 Garden Party of the ACLU of Southern California, the legal rights organization. Vidal, in a wheelchair and in failing health, attended as the guest of Stanley and Betty Sheinbaum, on whose Los Angeles estate the annual fundraiser was held. As the speechwriter of the event, I was tied up making sure that the emcee had the right cue cards, but by the time fellow Board member Steve Rohde started the auction, I sensed my chance to approach Vidal.

Among the items that Steve auctioned were the original artwork of editorial cartoons, collectible sports items, signed copies of Vidal's books, and lunches with celebrities.

"Mr. Vidal," I said, taking the seat next to his wheelchair, "I hope you don't mind, but could you autograph this script? It's one of my favorite films, and you predicted so much of what's happened since then."

Set at a political convention, *The Best Man* is a contest between a grandstanding conservative candidate played by Cliff Robertson (a combination of Richard Nixon and Robert Kennedy, whom Vidal despised), and a smart but overly contemplative candidate played by Henry Fonda (an Adlai Stevenson type). Brittle, incisive, and prescient, the 1960 play and its better 1964 film predicted the schism that, half a century later, dangerously divides America.

Vidal barely acknowledged me as he took my proffered pen. He paused. At that moment the auctioneer announced the next item: private lunch with Ramona Ripston, who was then the dynamic Executive Director of the ACLU of Southern California. Vidal poised my pen atop the script, nodded to the stage to indicate the auctioneer, looked me in the eyes and said, "Bid." At the time I had known Ramona for some twenty years, ever since she, her Deputy Director Liz Schroeder, and future Los Angeles Mayor Antonio Villaraigosa conspired to bring me onto her Board on the recommendation of John Roberts, Executive Director of the ACLU of Massachusetts, where I had previously served. In other words, it was the 501(C)4 version of being drafted.

"Bid?" I said.

"If you want me to sign," Vidal said, "bid."

So I did. Someone countered.

"Raise it," he said. I couldn't tell if the twinkle in his eyes came from his sense of humor or his second scotch.

So I raised. And again. When the auctioneer's gavel came down and awarded me lunch with Ramona, Vidal signed. "Thank you," I said. Then, as he automatically started to pocket my pen, all bets and bids were off. "Gimme my pen," I said, and grabbed it out of his hand. He said nothing further, but I had my Gore Vidal story.

There is actually an uncomfortable epilogue. It seems that Vidal attended the 2010 Garden Party thinking he was going to receive an award. Our new Executive Director, Hector Villaga, rectified this the next year and made an appropriate fuss. Vidal accepted graciously and then began to speak. After a few moments, he began to ramble, and the audience started to make that kind of uncomfortable sound that you can't describe but you know it when you hear it. The emcee didn't know what to do; you can't interrupt Gore Vidal. Suddenly I remembered how the White House Press Secretary breaks in and ends a Presidential press conference. I took the off-stage microphone—Vidal was using a hand mic—and said, "Thank you, Mr. Vidal." The audience applauded, Vidal was wheeled off, and nobody was embarrassed. He died the following July.

* * *

We were interviewing Gene Simmons, of the rock group KISS, for the A&E *Biography* of Stan Lee. Gene was born in Israel and said he learned to speak English, in part, from reading the Marvel comics that Stan wrote. Thus he was excited years later when Marvel published a KISS comic book. Not only that, for the occasion, Simmons and his band partners visited the printing plant where the first issue was being run off and pricked their fingers to put a few drops of their blood into the ink, thereby being able to say that they had—well, you get the idea. Simmons was funny and approachable during the interview so, as we finished, I asked for his autograph. Instead of a piece of paper, however, I handed him a tongue depressor. He broke up laughing and said it was the first time anybody had ever asked him to sign one.[40]

* * *

---

40 Simmons' tongue has a legendary length. And you know what they say.

Time Marches On

IN HOLLYWOOD they say that there are five ages of man, and they go like this:

> Who is Nat Segaloff?
> Get me Nat Segaloff.
> We need a Nat Segaloff type.
> We need a young Nat Segaloff.
> Who is Nat Segaloff?

Apropos the third one, Charles Nelson Reilly used to tell about the time he heard that a producer was looking for a "Charles Nelson Reilly type." Curious as to why he, Charles Nelson Reilly, hadn't been called about the part, he headed down to where the auditions were being held and presented himself, only to be told that he wasn't right for the role.

A strangely related case occurs when actors audition themselves out of a role. Leonard Nimoy talked about this when he, John de Lancie, and I were on a break from recording one of our Alien Voices® audiobooks. Leonard explained how some directors don't have a clear idea of how they want a role to be cast or played, so they invite a succession of actors to come in and read for it in the hope of clarifying their concept. "I did it this way and that," Leonard said of one audition at the start of his career, well before *Star Trek*, "and the director and I finally found a way to play the role that worked for both of us. And then guess what? I didn't get the part. I had spent all that time helping him decide exactly what he wanted, and then it turned out that what he wanted wasn't me."

Auditioning is a horrible process except that there really isn't an alternative. Said Richard Attenborough, who had just directed the ultimate audition piece *A Chorus Line*, "It's a terrible thing. It really is a terrible thing. I mean, I'm an actor and if I'm gonna do an audition, I'm gonna do a bit of Galsworthy or a bit of Oscar Wilde, and I've rehearsed it for months. I know it backwards and exactly how I'm gonna play it. I know how I'm gonna stand, I know everything I'm gonna do. But if you are a gypsy [musical theatre dancer-singer], you come and stand in front of the choreographer, and he says, 'Do so-and-so and so-and-so and two flipbacks, all right, do it.' And you have to do it. You have ninety seconds to do it in. And in that ninety seconds you're on or you're off. Some of them may have waited three years to get that opportunity, and what have they got [for a working career]? Ten years? Eleven years? Twelve years? They're like athletes, they're like tennis players. They're over at thirty-one or thirty-two. It's an obscene process. I don't know how else you do it, but it's a terrible, cruel process."

They say you know within thirty seconds of stepping into the audition room if you have a chance, and then you have to stay there anyway in case lightning strikes or you impress the director or casting consultant that you're good for some other role if not the one you showed up for. Some of the time they just want your "look" and figure the acting can come later. I had a friend who was always being cast as trust fund babies and evil preppies, which was a tragedy because his range was far greater than that and his professionalism was top-notch, but he was also painfully handsome and well-poised and his aesthetic worked against him. Strange problem, no?[41]

I wrote before of how director Arthur Penn asked even those actors who gave superb auditions to come back so he could make sure the first time wasn't a fluke. He also had a trick when casting kids, such as the character of "Rufus" in Tad Mosel's play *All the Way Home* based on James Agee's novel *A Death in the Family*. Rather than have the kids stand on stage and recite a practiced speech, he had them explore the set while he pitched them questions and they answered while playing with

---

41 Fortunately, Fate intervened and they started making TV shows about gorgeous vampires. He got hired as a series regular.

the props. It drove stage mothers nuts, but it allowed Arthur to test how the kids *behaved* rather than how they *performed.*

Often there is tension when actor and director differ on how to play a role; in film, the director wins if only because he chooses the takes. If he's conciliatory, he may shoot an alternate version the way the actor insists on doing it, but the actor can never be sure that the footage will be used—or, for that matter, whether there is even any film in the camera. I learned a term once on a shoot where the public relations director of the location we were using insisted on being interviewed. I knew we'd never use it but we were backed into a diplomatic corner because this flack held the key to our access, so I nodded to the cameraman to roll tape. "Shall we do it M-O-T?" he asked. I'd never heard the term before. I was familiar with "M-O-S," which means "mitt out sound," industry lingo supposedly coined by a German cameraman for shooting without recording audio. "What's M-O-T?" I asked. The cameraman drew me aside and confided, "It means 'mitt out tape.'" And that's how I interviewed the guy: with nothing in the camera.

For an independent picture called *Family Honor* about, what else, the Mob, the distributor sent the star, Anthony Page, to Boston and it was my job to book appearances for him. It was one of his first films and few members of the press were interested, even as eyewash. As it happened, Tony had served a stretch in a penitentiary and didn't mind talking about it, so I called the warden at one of the state's medium security prisons and arranged a seminar. The actor told some of the inmates about being in the joint, going straight, and becoming an actor, and *that* became a story worthy of press coverage. (Sadly, Tony died at age 41 just as he was getting more work.)

Death is not the greatest liability in Hollywood. It's age. It's not uncommon for a producer to want a particular actor only to learn that he, but usually she, looks too old to play the part. Now that high-definition digital has taken over the movies, every age line shows, but not as much as the pancake makeup applied to cover it. The life span of a leading actress these days is seven years from age 18 to 25. In other words, as with so much in Hollywood, just when you get good at what you do, they won't let you do it anymore.

Not so long ago the first rite of passage was television—not doing it, but seeing your first movie turn up on it. That was when there was a two-year window between silver screen and boob tube. The first movie I ever publicized was *Love Story*, the schmaltz-fest about a twenty-five-year-old girl who dies. I had worked on the New England premiere at the end of 1970 that landed me a job with Paramount's field agency and didn't looked back until it aired on ABC on October 1, 1972. I felt old. Actors tell me the same thing. These days, of course, by the time you get home from seeing it at the multiplex it's on Netflix.

It's also disturbing, but in a different way, to see dead people. By this I mean actors you worked with who have died, yet their film appearances live. You expect it in old movies, but not pictures that you yourself made. I feel this way about more people than I care to remember. You know when people say, "They may be dead but their work survives," or "We can always enjoy watching them for as long as film exists." Small comfort. When Jimmy Stewart talked about "pieces of time" he meant the film, not the fun you had sitting around between takes or swapping stories over wrap beers. I will never hear Slim Pickens tell his cowboy limericks again, or Dom DeLuise perform the joke about the lady lion and the horny chimpanzee, or director Arthur Hiller telling about the time when they were making *Man of La Mancha* and Peter O'Toole—well, you had to be there. None of these made it into the films they were shooting or the interviews they gave. They exist now as precious memories, embroidered a little perhaps, but alive forever as private time with public figures.

Future Schlock

WHAT IS THE future of movies? I don't mean "Hollywood" Becaue, the way things are going, Hollywood is not the future of movies. Everywhere is. For the first time since the movies were invented, anybody can make one. Portable digital cameras and laptop editing programs have turned every back yard into a location and every family rec room into a soundstage. Three hundred thousand of them are uploaded *every day* to YouTube, Daily Motion, Vimeo, Twitch, Veoh, LiveLeak, and similar video sharing websites. The problem is no longer how to make movies. The problem is getting people to see yours.

Hollywood initially solved that challenge by monopolizing production, distribution, and exhibition. For thirty years from 1918 to 1948 it was Hollywood's way or no way at all, but the U.S. Department of Justice broke that up with the Paramount et al Consent Decree[42] divorcing theatres from studios. It took another twenty years for the film companies to find ways around the Consent Decree and not only produce and distribute films, but put upstart independent competitors out of business by absorbing them. In 2016 there were 336 films released in America

---

[42] In 1938 the Justice Department brought anti-trust action against Paramount and the other studios that both produced, distributed, and exhibited films claiming vertical integration and monopoly. By 1948 a Consent Decree (out-of-court settlement) was reached divorcing the theatre chains from the studios. Since then, new vertically integrated corporations have emerged but the DOJ has no apparent interest in pursuing anti-trust action against them. In essence, they are saying that if you put a video on YouTube you have just as much access to the public as a major film company booking a new movie into 5,000 theatres. I disagree.

that qualified for Academy Award consideration.[43] About half were from the six major studios (Disney, Paramount, Sony, Warner Bros., Universal, and Twentieth Century Fox) and the rest were from independent distribution companies. That appears to be a robust competitive market --until one realizes that most of the independent releases never played more than the one week they needed to qualify for Oscars, while the major titles ran for months and accounted for the lion's share of Hollywood's $11.5 billion gross. Theatre figures are equally misleading. At this writing there are 40,759 screens in America,[44] half of which (21,471) are controlled by ten chains.[45] The other 19,288 are independently owned. While this appears equitable, independent exhibitors who lack the muscle of owning scores of screens are at a disadvantage when they bargain for product and are at an even greater disadvantage when they negotiate an equitable settlement of their rental agreements. The more screens you control, the more power you have over the distributor (because you're holding his ticket money). By any calculation, independent films have limited market access. Even when they do gain access to a chain cinema, their distributor may be forced to yield to the theatre's financial terms in exchange for the prime booking.

The commercial tension between independent and major film companies is paralleled by aesthetic tension. After a decade of realistic but often depressing subjects from roughly 1965 to 1975, movies again were made with happy, if artificial, endings. Often endings were reshot and tacked on after test audiences said they wanted a more upbeat resolution, even if nothing in the story led up to it. Such endings generally involved dispatching the villain not through legal comeuppance, but with a bang.[46] It's important to please audiences, but it's also important to reflect recognizable human behavior. Not any more; nowadays when a villain is killed, audiences wait for him to spring back to life for one last attack on

---

43 Source: AMPAS

44 Source for number of screens: National Association of Theatre Owners, 2015 survey. (www.natoonline.org/data/us-movie-screens/)

45 Chains: Statista, the Statistics Portal: https://www.statista.com/statistics/188565/north-american-movie-theater-circuits-by-number-of-screens/

46 The classic case is *Fatal Attraction* (1987). SPOILER: The filmmaker's ending had the villain, Glenn Close, commit suicide but incriminate her illicit lover, Michael Douglas, for her murder. Preview audiences carped, so the studio changed the ending so Close is killed by Douglas's wife, Anne Archer. The film made millions.

the hero. Viewers are accustomed to being set up for a sequel as the last scene slowly reveals a plot point that they forgot an hour ago but which now looms large before the end credits roll.

There are no more sequels, there are franchises. Franchises are sequels by another name, yet they resolve nothing because doing so would end the franchise. Or they call a film a "reboot." A reboot is a remake. Admit it. Because the international market now accounts for two-thirds of a mega-budget film's business, storylines have to be simplified and dialogue reduced to a minimum. This has led to a resurgence of character "types" (read: stereotypes) because preview audiences, raised on the instant gratification of television, regard character development as boring. The founding moguls might be upset that the America they idealized in thousands of films has now been corrupted to appease a global market. They wanted to turn a profit, sure, but they wanted to do it in a way that upheld their personal ideals. I recall asking one of the top people at United Artists—at the time the most artistically free film company in the business—if there was anything that UA would ever refuse to make a film about. He thought for a moment and said, "Assassinating a President." I was proud that a studio I once worked for had limits.

The thoughtful, often experimental who came of age in what is now considered the modern halcyon decade from the mid-1960s to mid-1970s probably cringe at the cynicism that has come to pass for screen entertainment. Super heroes? Comic book movies? Vampires? Zombies? Rom-Coms? Remakes instead of originals? These are fine for escapism, but they now dominate major release schedules. How do they give anyone the tools to navigate the human condition? Isn't that what art is supposed to do, and not just kill time? Or is it all about, "Make you laugh, make you cry, kiss your twenty bucks goodbye"?

If this sounds like the protestations of a bitter old Don Quixote tilting at celluloid (now digital) windmills, ask yourself how many big-budget blockbuster movies you've really loved lately, or whether you just left the theatre and grabbed a sandwich. How do you identify with a character in danger when you know the danger is CGI and the character is a mo-cap digital image?

This is why independent cinema holds hope. Until the mid-1970s there was a vital art and independent cinema in America. Small theatres played small films and both companies could exist on small profits.

Quite often the people who proved themselves in the indie genres got hired by the Hollywood studios to make bigger films, new filmmakers entered at the bottom of the ladder, and the creative ladder continued. Beginning in the 1990s with the sale of the feisty indie company Miramax to Disney, the major film companies saw that the independents were, dollar for dollar, doing better than they were, so they bought them hoping to corner the entire market. It never occurred to them that the indies couldn't throw off enough profit to justify the purchase and, in time, all of them were either folded or absorbed. In other words, in wanting to own all the golden eggs, Hollywood throttled the goose that laid them. The few independent producers and distributors that are left (there are practically no independent arthouse exhibitors, although they're out there) must compete with the majors for screen time. Fat chance. Hollywood may be the only major American industry that devours its young.

Where do we go from here? We go back. If thoughtful independent cinema is going to survive it needs to be separate from mainstream cinema. If it appeals mostly to grownups and the intelligentsia, then it must be in places that are accessible to that audience. Just as shopping malls play classical music to discourage young people from hanging out there, so can indie cinema stick to indie attractions to define themselves. It's called branding. They need parking, reasonable ticket prices, visible ushers, sound systems that don't blast, high-quality projected image, reasonable food at concession stands, no pre-show advertising, no smart phones, and whatever else it takes to pry audiences out of the house and back to the theatre. Young people go to the movies for community; grownups go for film. Some small circuits such as the Arclight and Alamo Draft House understand this. As the indie circuit re-establishes itself, attractions will be curated, brands will emerge, and a viable economic profile will develop. Beyond that, it will be up to the movies themselves. It will take a while to come about.

Many of the filmmakers I've interviewed over the years faced this realization. One of the first to see into the future was a man who'd visualized it by creating the effects for *Blade Runner, Silent Running, Star Trek: The Motion Picture, Close Encounters of the Third Kind* and the one that blew the door open for all of them, *2001: A Space Odyssey*.

When we met, Douglas Trumbull had just made *Brainstorm*, a troubled MGM production that first lost its female star (Natalie Wood), then had the new head of production (David Begelman) try to cash the movie for the insurance, and finally strangle it with poor bookings and minimal advertising support (it was supposed to be shown in 70mm and ended up in 35mm). After *Brainstorm*, which came and went in 1983, Trumbull became a technical innovator. First he moved into interactive motion-controlled amusement park rides (like *Back to the Future* at Universal City Studios), then he ventured into ShowScan, a 70mm film process that is projected at 60 frames per second instead of the customary 30 fps, giving the viewer an immersive experience in a near-grainless image. He was at the forefront of video technology applied to cinema and has been developing 120 fps digital video cameras that capture action as accurately as the human eye, then combine it with standard 30 fps video and even 3D. An artist (mother's influence) as well as an engineer (father's influence), Trumbull unifies creativity and commerce. He was already exploring those avenues when we spoke thirty years before they burst on the scene.

"Entertainment is going to continue to evolve," he explained in 1983. "The motion picture industry hasn't evolved since the late forties because of the Consent Decree and the restriction of ownership of theatres by studios [has reduced competition]. There's no technological competition in the movie industry. It is being overtaken by electronic media which has tremendous ability to distribute, edit, manipulate electronically all kinds of imagery and there's no question in my mind that you're going to have wall screen TV—flat solid state, liquid crystal displays, or plasma displays, or whatever it's going to take to get flat TV, that's a matter of manufacturing and marketing. The technology already exists so there's no mystery to that. I think if you go to a theatre it'd better be spectacular. It'll be bigger, wider, brighter, more realistic, giant stereo sound. It better be a dramatic, theatrical showmanship event, otherwise I'm going to stay home and I think everybody else feels generally the same way. So you're going to get that kind of division between what's a theatrical film and what goes on TV."

I pointed out to Trumbull that the head of General Cinema, which at the time owned 1200 screens, mostly in suburban shopping malls, had told me that 70mm is a gimmick, Dolby stereo is a gimmick, and that, "If you have the film they [the audience] want to see, you can show it in the toilet." Not surprisingly, Trumbull took issue. "People will demand spectacular productions with Dolby stereo, six track, and 70mm prints because if they don't get it they're going to watch television."[47] And since then they have.

Francis Ford Coppola, whose operatic visions go from the *Godfather* trio to *Apocalypse Now* and *Bram Stoker's Dracula* to *Rumblefish*, is also a visionary. As the critics were leaving the sometimes-tense press conference for his then-new *Apocalypse Now* on August 11, 1979, he was surrounded at the front of the room by some of the younger critics. The speakers were turned off, but I kept my tape recorder running and picked up, in a brief few moments, his predictions for the future of cinema, and damned if it hasn't come true. (This has never been published):

"I have been very interested in the future, in how not only television but movies can be made. I really do sense a major revolution in the way motion pictures can be made and in the technology and the control and who controls them. What areas they can even dream of. You realize that most filmmakers are right in there. They are told they can write, 'Here is Jack, here is Jill, Jill likes Jack.' That's how much you're allowed to work with in motion pictures, which is a form that, that you can do anything. You can make sixteen-hour movies that would work, that people would just to go for the weekend and be in a nice place and see three hours at a time. You could do anything. We're expected to make movies a certain way: you've got to root for the characters, you've got to crank up to a big finale and have a clear denouement that everyone has seen before. That's why the innovative work is so difficult—until a couple years later when they say, 'Oh, yeah, that movie's good.' The areas that I have been working in are, I want to run a movie studio. We want to make our own pictures. I make films for my audiences but I always want to give my audiences the best it can be, not just serve them up the same plate of food warmed up in a microwave oven every time. Having a character to root for is a very important part of many movies but there are many ways to do it. If you say that all films must have a principal character, that's the thinking

---

47 General Cinema Corporation went under in 2002.

of a lot of studio heads, and a lot of movies you would never get made if you adhered to that rule."[48]

Go back and read it again. In a few short minutes, Coppola described what became the modern trend of binge-watching, the rise of anti-heroes such as mobsters, vampires, and serial killers in television shows, the emergence of video streaming services that challenge the distribution system, and a few innovative filmmakers (Steven Soderbergh, David Fincher) who reject traditional narrative structure. They don't work for the old studios, but for the new ones like Netflix, Hulu, and Amazon.

Like Coppola, cinematographer-director Haskell Wexler saw changes coming, and his emotions about it were mixed. "The primary consumer of dramatic film material is television," he said in 1986, "and TV is set to reach the lowest common denominator. You want to sell as much as you can to as many people as you can. That includes television news. The first thing [the TV executives] look at when they get in each morning is the ratings reports. So what we artists have to work on is what these people in power select to put out. Unfortunately, what [the studios] put out is sold to television. Most scripts are built with commercial breaks in them. Writers sense that you must grab the audience. It's almost computerized. Writers may be writing other things, but they know what will sell and what won't sell. Movies about revenge, for example, where you knock the guy down at the beginning and then he comes back, that's all they're making now."

Aside from missing how the rise of home video would practically doom television sales for theatrical motion pictures, Wexler nailed it. In a sense, movies and TV shows did become computerized. Thanks to a slew of "how to" books, screenwriters know that reveals and plot points are expected to happen on pages 15, 33, 50, 66, and so forth. Audiences become trained to expect certain things at certain times, like Pavlov's dog. And if audiences don't, then production executives do. Stories that fit the mold get made. Those that are too original do not.

---

48 During the press conference Coppola had facetiously said, "Now that I've done *Apocalypse Now*, I want to do something *really* hard." After the laugh died down, he added, "Maybe a little love story." The next day, a studio insider told me, he asked for a copy of Lawrence Durrell's mammoth *Alexandria Quartet*. What he eventually made was *One From the Heart* (1982) whose critical and commercial failure bankrupted his ambitious Zoëtrope Studios.

"I was told that a script had to have three original scenes in it," Robby Benson said in his soft voice. He and his father had just co-written, and he had starred in, the film *One on One* (1977) about a young basketball jock. He was trying to get behind the camera. "'Only three original scenes?' I asked [the head of production]. 'What's wrong with having *all* original scenes?' The guy said, 'No, three is enough. The audience isn't expecting any more.'"

Not only has movie content become standardized over the years, movie costs have entered the discussion. Now critics review the budget as well as the picture. This was Warren Beatty's beef after *Ishtar* was released in 1987. At an unconfirmed cost of $51 million plus another $10 million in marketing (and with Beatty, Dustin Hoffman, and writer-director Elaine May reportedly receiving $12.5 million) *Ishtar* needed to gross at least $150 million just to breakeven. It flatlined at $14.3 million domestic.

John Landis, whose *Animal House* was one of the most profitable films ever made, followed by *The Blues Brothers*, which was one of the most (at the time) costly, put a peg in the subject. "A movie costs what a movie costs," he said in our 1980 interview. "Period. The economic thing becomes a sore point with me. If you're gonna make *Ben-Hur*, it's gonna cost a lot of money. A movie costs what a movie costs and economics should never enter into whether you like it or not. If you look at a painting, I don't think you go, 'I dunno, Rauschenberg had a pretty good quality canvas, I can't like it as much.' It's very bizarre. 'Is that oil or acrylic?' When you look at a sculpture you don't think about how much the bronze costs. It costs what it costs. It's the work you have to judge by itself. Also, I think the press has a basic ignorance of the realities of film production. Hollywood did, for a while, too. I think Hollywood was really shocked to, all of a sudden, turn around and, in one year, find that costs had gone up four hundred percent. *Animal House* made hundreds of millions, so their profit margin is enormous and it only cost 2.6 million, whereas in a *Blues Brothers*, they have to make more money to recoup 'cause it's more expensive. You forget that *The Wizard of Oz* did not make money until 1955 when it was sold to television. *The Maltese Falcon* was a failure economically. I don't think economics are the issue over whether you like a movie or not. A classic case for me was *2001* which got some of the worst reviews I ever read, and that's a seminal motion picture, But

Pauline Kael called it 'monumentally unimaginative.' What movie was she watching?"

Douglas Trumbull, Francis Ford Coppola, Haskell Wexler, Robbie Benson, and John Landis. Five diverse filmmakers, but each of them was as concerned about the commerce of cinema as they were with its art. In light of what has happened to the American film industry since these exchanges—tent pole blockbusters, franchises, remakes/reboots, and sequels—each of them was, to varying degrees, correct. If you look at the grosses, they're impressive, but if you divide them by the price of tickets, they're not. The fact is that ticket sales are down even though grosses are up because of increased prices, not because more people are going to the movies. Major releases do indeed seem to be formulaic, and people have indeed gravitated toward home theatre. Not the broadcast networks of old, but the premium channels like HBO and Showtime and streaming services like Netflix. Now it's young adults and little kids who go to the real movies; grown-ups too frequently opt to stay at home because of talkers, texters, cell phones, and the high cost of popcorn. Even many of the cinema's best filmmakers now find a more generous welcome and greater freedom on television.

I still believe that a large theatre with a quiet, involved audience is the best way to see a movie. Movies are a group experience that generate not only a shared reaction but a shared community. Watching them at home or on a portable device defeats the purpose of mass entertainment. Hollywood may be dead, but the dreams that built Hollywood continue to inspire, seduce, and satisfy. What we need now is for them to prevail.

Nat Segaloff
Biography

NAT SEGALOFF IS a writer-producer-journalist. He covered the film industry for *The Boston Herald* but has also variously been a studio publicist (Fox, UA, Columbia), college teacher (Boston University, Boston College), and broadcaster (ABC, Group W, CBS, Storer). He is the author of fifteen books including *Hurricane Billy: The Stormy Life and Films of William Friedkin*, *Arthur Penn: American Director*, and *Final Cuts: The Last Films of 50 Great Directors* in addition to career monographs on Walon Green, Paul Mazursky and John Milius. His writing has appeared in such varied periodicals as *Film Comment*, *Written By*, *International Documentary*, *Animation Magazine*, *The Christian Science Monitor*, *Time Out* (US), *MacWorld*, and *American Movie Classics Magazine*. He was also senior reviewer for AudiobookCafe.com and contributing writer to *Moving Pictures* magazine. His *The Everything® Etiquette Book*, *The Everything® Trivia Book* and *The Everything® Tall Tales, Legends & Outrageous Lies Book* are in multiple printings for Adams Media Corp.

As a TV writer-producer, Segaloff helped perfect the format and create episodes for A&E's flagship *Biography* series. His distinctive productions include episodes on John Belushi, Stan Lee, Larry King, Shari Lewis & Lamb Chop, and Darryl F. Zanuck. He wrote and co-produced the *Rock 'n' Roll Moments* music series for The Learning Channel/Malcolm Leo Productions, and has written and/or produced programming for New World, Disney, Turner Classic Movies, and USA Networks. He is co-creator/co-producer of the documentary *Judgment Day* with Grosso-Jacobson Communications Corp. for HBO.

His extraterrestrial endeavors include the cheeky sequel to the Orson Welles "Invasion From Mars" radio hoax, "When Welles Collide," which featured a *Star Trek®* cast. It was produced by L.A. Theatre Works and has become a Halloween tradition on National Public Radio. In 1996 he formed the multi-media production company Alien Voices® with actors John de Lancie and Leonard Nimoy and produced five best-selling, fully dramatized audio plays for Simon & Schuster: *The Time Machine, Journey to the Center of the Earth, The Lost World, The Invisible Man* and *The First Men in the Moon*, all of which feature *Star Trek®* casts. Additionally, his teleplay for *The First Men in the Moon* was the first-ever TV/Internet simulcast and was presented live by The Sci-Fi Channel. He has also written narrative concerts for the Los Angeles Philharmonic, celebrity events, is a script consultant, and was a contributing writer to *Moving Pictures* magazine. He now contributes show business fiction to Nikki Finke's celebrated website, HollywoodDementia.com

Nat is the co-author of *The Waldorf Conference*, a dramatic comedy about the secret 1947 meeting of studio moguls that began the Hollywood Blacklist. The play had its all-star world premiere at L.A. Theatre Works and was acquired for production by Warner Bros. He produced a subsequent production (okay, a "reboot") to benefit the Hollywood ACLU and the Writers Guild Foundation, and has also produced such other celebrity events as a public reading of censored books and a recreation of the classic anti-HUAC broadcast, "Hollywood Fights Back." He was staff producer for The Africa Channel, wrote the stage play *Closets* (produced at Massachusetts' Gloucester Stage Company), and is co-writer for the popular public radio word/game show "Says You!" after having been a frequent guest panelist.

His previous book is *A Lit Fuse: The Provocative Life of Harlan Ellison* (NESFA Press). Before that and this book he published *Mr. Huston/ Mr. North: Life, Death, and the Making of John Huston's Last Film; Final Cuts: The Last Films of 50 Great Directors; Stirling Silliphant: The Fingers of God;* and *Screen Saver: Private Stories of Public Hollywood,* for which this book is the sequel (okay, franchise), all from Bear Manor Media.

He is now looking for work.

Index

Numbers in **bold** indicate photographs

A&E 8-9, 10-16, 118, 123, 126, 137, 151
Abbott, Andrew 52
Alexandria Quartet 148
Alien Voices 44, 138, 152
All the Way Home 139-140
Allen, Karen 114-116
Allen, Woody 66, 103
Alonzo, John 36-37
Amarillo Slim 129
And Now for Something Completely Different 50
Anderson, Ernie 98
Animal House 1, 96, 113-116, 117, 118-119, 120, 149
Apocalypse Now 30, 147, 148
Armstrong, Louis 98
Arness, James 15
At Long Last Love 106
Attenborough, Richard 34-35, **87**, 139
Austin, David 75, 76, 77
Autry, Gene 95-96

Bacall, Lauren 100
"Back in the Saddle Again" 95-96
Baker, Jack 75, 76
Bakshi, Ralph 66, 132
Bambi 131-132
Bambi, The Story and the Film 132
Bambi: A Life in the Wood 131
Beatty, Warren 105, 149
Begelman, David 126, 146
Belafonte, Harry x
Belushi, Jim 10
Belushi, John 9-10, 116, 118, 151
Benson, Robby 149, 150
Best Man, The 135-136
Biography 8-11, 15-16, 23, 25, 118, 123, 126-127, 137
Birth of a Nation, The 105
Black Stallion, The 65

Blatty, William Peter 3-4, 100
Blues Brothers, The 116, 117, 149
Bogdanovich, Peter 105, 106, 108
Boreman, Linda 57-63, **78**
Born on the Fourth of July 29
Brewer, Roy x
Bridges, James 24, 69-70, 96, 128, 130
Brighton Rock 35
Brink's Job, The 25, 29-33, **80**
Brooks, Mel 122
Bruce, Lenny 6
Burton, Tim 100
Burtt, Ben 43-44
Byrne, Terry 130

Cain, Jess 49
California Split 129
Cameron, James 13
Carradine, Robert 99
Chambers, John 64-65
Chambers, Marilyn 59
Charlie's Angels 53-54
Chew, Richard 68
Chickens! 47-51, **81**
China Syndrome, The 24
Chorus Line, A 34, 35, 139
Claflin, Larry 94-95
Cleese, John 50
Codianni, Jean Louise 11
Cohen, Leonard 73
Collins, Monica 28
Connery, Sean **89**
Coppola, Francis Ford 147-148, 150
Cronenberg, David 55
Curtis, Jamie Lee 102
Cushing, Peter 39-40, **82**

Dahl, Roald 100
Daniel, Sean 120
Davis, Tom 118

Day, Doris ix
De Lancie, John 138, 152
De Laurentiis, Dino 29, 32, 33, 96
De Niro, Robert 22, 38, 110
Dean, James 69-70
Deep Throat 57-63
Dekom, Peter 99
DeLuise, Dom ix, xi, 65, 141
Depp, Johnny 100
Disney, Walt 3, 12, 17, 42-43, 44, 124, 125-126, 131-132, 143, 145, 152
Don Juan in Hell 45
Downey, Sr., Robert 119-120
Dreyfuss, Richard 22-23, 38, 93
Drizzle, The 96
Duffy, Sherman Reilly 128
Duncan, Sandy 45-46

Earthquake 69
Ebert, Roger 72-73, 105, 106
Egan, Eddie 83, 110-111
Emperor, The 94
Evening Magazine 18-28, 30-32, 71, **79, 80, 84,** 90, 92, 121
Exorcist, The 1-4, 25, 30, 111

Falk, Peter 25, 30, **80**
Family Honor 140
Fatal Attraction 143
Fawcett, Farrah xi, 53
Ferrigno, Lou 13
First Men in the Moon, The 44, 152
First Nudie Musical, The 24, **84**
Flash Gordon (1980) 1, 2
Fogerty, John 67
Fonda, Jane 24, 38
For the Love of Movies 72
Forbes, David 123
Ford, Gerald 21
Ford, John xii, 65
Forsythe, John 54
Fraker, William 36, 37
Frankenheimer John 29
French Connection, The 25, 29, 52, 53, **83,** 110, 111

Friedkin, Johnny 122
Friedkin, William 3, 4, 25, 29-33, 52-53, 65, **80,** 110, 111-112, 122

Gabler, Neal 3
Gelbart, Larry viii, x, 5-6
Geller, Bruce 15, 128-129
Ghost (1990) 35
Giorgio, Tony 128-129
Goldberg, Whoopi 35
Gone with the Wind 40, 41
Graves, Peter 15-16
Greatest, The (A&E Biography) 23-24, **84**
Griffith, D. W. 3, 105
Grodin, Charles vi, 102
Grossman, Gary H. 8, 9, 11, 16
Grosso, Sonny 29, **83,** 110-111
Guarnaccia, Phyllis 95
Guinness, Alec 23
Gunton, Dick 74

Hackman, Gene 52-53
Hagler, Marvin 110
Halloween 102
Harlan, Robin 44
Harris, Linda 27
Hecht, Ben 128
"Helan Gor" 2, 83
Hello Dolly **88,** 124
Hersey, Dana 28
Heston, Charlton **80,** 114, 129
Hill, Debra 102
Hillier, Bill 18, 19, 21, 22
Hitchcock, Alfred xii, 54, 70, 72
Hoffman, Dustin 5-7, **82,** 149
"Hollywood Censorship Wars, The" 9
Hombre 37
Houghton, Tom 22, 26
House That Dripped Blood, The 39
Houseman, John 45
How Green Was My Valley 65
Hud 36, 37
Hudson, Bob 94
Huntsman, Paul 44

Hurricane Billy 25, 111, 151
Hurricane, The 96
Huston, John 98, 152
Hyde-Pierce, David 101

Irwin, Mark 54, 55
Ishtar 6, 7, 149

Jacklin, Judith 9
Jackson, Kate 53-54
Jackson, Larry xii, 48, 134-135
John Belushi: Funny You Should Ask 9-10
Johnson, Tom 11, 12-13
Johnston, Ollie 131-132
Jones, Sarah 118
Jorgensen, Randy 112
Judgment Day 111, 152
Julius Caesar 114

Kael, Pauline 105, 150
Kazan, Elia 13
Keane, Clif 94-95
Kenney, Doug 113, 114, 118
Kermode, Mark 4, 52
King, Larry 11-13, 153
Kurlander, Dick 28

Ladd, Cheryl 53-54
LaMonte, Christine xii, 1, 2
LaMotta, Jake 110
Landis, John **86**, 113, 116-119, 120, 149, 150
Laquidara, Charles 49
Larry King: Talk of Fame 11-13, 153
Larson, Jack 130
Last Tango in Paris 110
Lee, Stan 13-14, 137, 151
Leeds, Susan 48
Lemmon, Jack 24, 42
Lennick, Michael 54, 55-56, **79**
Lenny (1974) 6
Lewis, Shari 10-11, 13, 14, 151
Lilly, Toni 25, 30
Little Big Man 7

Lombard, Carole xii
Love Story ix, 141
Lovelace, Linda see Boreman, Linda
Lucas, George 50, 68, 94

MacDonald, Jimmy 42-43
Maltin, Leonard 24, 132
Mandel, Howie 35-36
Mangan, Maddie 40
Manker, Russell (Russ) 21, 121, 127
Marchiano, Larry 57, 58, 63
Marchiano, Linda see Boreman, Linda
Marshall, Garry 101
Martin, Mary 45-46
May, Elaine 149
Mayer, Louis B. 3, 126
Maynard, Dave 26
McDaniel, Hattie 40
Mcdonald, Gregory 130-131
McDowall, Roddy 65, 101
McGannon, Donald 19, 27
McQueen, Butterfly 40-41, **85**
Michaels, Lorne 10
Midnight Rider: The Gregg Allman Story 118
Milius, John 99, 100, 109
Miller, Chris 114-116
Monty Python 50
Morris, Oswald 45
Morrow, Vic 117
Mosely, Leonard 35
Movie Loft & Company 28, 90
Mr. and Mrs. Smith (1941) xii
Muhammad Ali 23
Murphy's Romance 36, 37-38

Nadell, Gerry 91
Nadell, Sue 14, 15
Needham, Hal 108
Never Forget 67-68
Newman, Paul 100, 103
Nimoy, Leonard ix, 67-68, 138-139, 152
Nixon, Richard 126, 134, 136
Nobles Gate 52-53

Norton, Elliot 46

Ochs, Meegan xii, 5
One from the Heart 148
One on One 149
Outrageous! 38-39

Pacino, Al 29
Page, Anthony 140
Palin, Michael 50
Pauken, Adam "Chip" 9, 11
Paul, Jennie 95-96
Peary, Gerald 72
Penn, Arthur viii, 7, 52-53, 64, 72, 139-140
Perdue, Frank 48
Perkins, Jack 9, 15
Perot, Ross 11
Peter Pan 45-46
Peters, Brock 110
Peters, Rick 76-77
PM Magazine see Evening Magazine
Polonsky, Abraham x
Poughkeepsie Shuffle, The 52
Price, Frank 135

Radner, Gilda 9
Radnitz, Robert 67-68, 86, 89
Raging Bull 110
Rampling, Charlotte 89, 109
Real Paper, The 28
Reilly, Charles Nelson 138
Reno, Kelly 65
Reynolds, Burt ix, xi, 106
Ripston, Ramona 136
Ritt, Martin 36-38, **87, 89**
Rogoff, Ken 40, 49, 114
Rohde, Steve 136
Ross, Harold 104
Russell, Craig 38-39
Rydell, Mark 65, **85**, 124

Salier, Edward 12
Saroyan, Lucy 108-109
Saturday Night Live 9-10, 24, 96, 113

Saunders, Gus 92-93
Savage, John 22
Scanners 55
Schickel, Richard 47, 48, 50, 105
Schiller, Tom 10
Schlöndorff, Volker 69
Schwarzenegger, Arnold 109
Sender, Marty 22, 24, **79**
September 30, 1955 69-70
Serpe, Ralph 29, 31
Shari Lewis & Lamb Chop 10-11, 13, 14, 151
Shelton, Ken 49, 71, 72, 74
Silliphant, Stirling 68, 123
Simmons, Gene 13, 137
Sinatra, Frank 111
Siskel, Gene 73, 106
Smidt, Clark 71-76, 91
Smith, Jaclyn 53-54
Sorcerer 24, 29, 30, 111
Southcombe, Bryan 109
Spellmeyer, Jim 74, 77
Stallone, Sylvester 133-134
Stan Lee: The ComiX-Man 13-14, 137, 151
Star Trek xi, 9, 138, 145, 152
Star Wars ix, 23, 33, 39, 43-44, 45, 68
Staying Alive 132-134
Stein, Gertrude 128
Stewart, James 108, 141
Stiller, Ben 5, 7, **82**
Streisand, Barbra 38, **88**, 124
Sturges, Preston 47, 50
Sullivan's Travels 47
Swarm, The 24
Syatt, Dick and Jane 57, 58, 93

Taxi Zum Klo (Taxi to the Toilet) 77
Thalberg, Irving xii
Thomas, Frank 131-132
Thomas, Richard 69-70
Tillson, Todd 11
Time Machine 9
Tin Drum, The 69
Toback, James 108-109

Tootsie 5-6
Towering Inferno, The 50, 68, 122
Travolta, John 133
Traynor, Charles 58-61, 63
Trumbull, Douglas 145-146, 150
Trump, Donald 115
Turner, Ted 11-12, 76
Twilight Zone: The Movie, The 117-118

Urban Cowboy 96

"Vanz Kant Danz" 67
Vidal, Gore 135-137
Villain, The 108
Vinton, Will 66-67, 132
Von Sydow, Max 1-2, 3, **83**

Ward, Jay 48, 126-127
Wasserman, Lew 1, 126
Weiss, Mike 98
Weller, Robb 8, 9, 16
Weller/Grossman Productions 8, 16
Welles, Orson 42, 72, 134, 135, 152
Wexler, Haskell 148, 150
Wexler, Norman 132-133
Whitlock, Albert 68-69
Widdoes, Jamie 114-116
Wilder, Gene ix, 81, 99-100
Williams, Billy Dee 103
Willy Wonka and the Chocolate Factory **81**, 99-100
Woman in Red, The 9
Wong Howe, James 36, 37
Wood, Frank E. 105
Woolf, Stacy 12

Young Torless 69
Young, Robin 22, 30, **79, 80**

Zaentz, Saul 67
Zanuck, Darryl F. 3, 16, 101, 123, 151
Zanuck, Richard D. 123
Zardoz **89**, 109
Zeller, Gary 54-56

Screen Saver Too: *Hollywood Strikes Back*

Made in the USA
Columbia, SC
08 March 2023